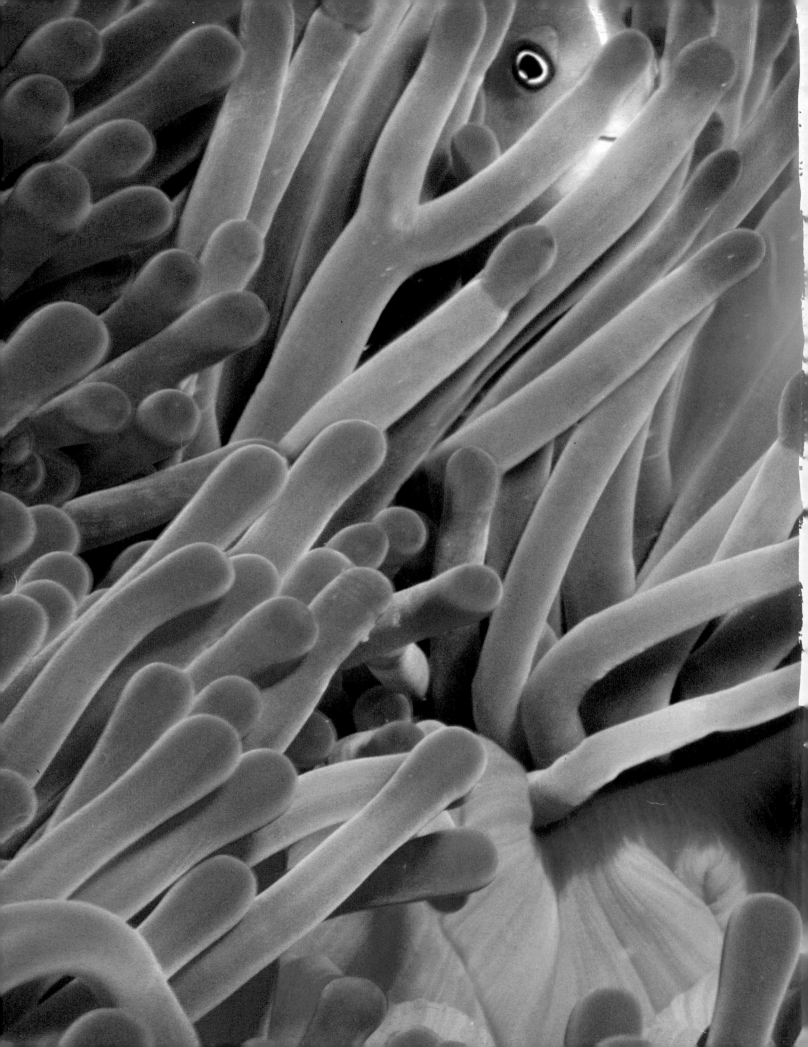

USBORNE
INTERNET-LINKED
MYSTERIES & MARVELS
OF
NATURE

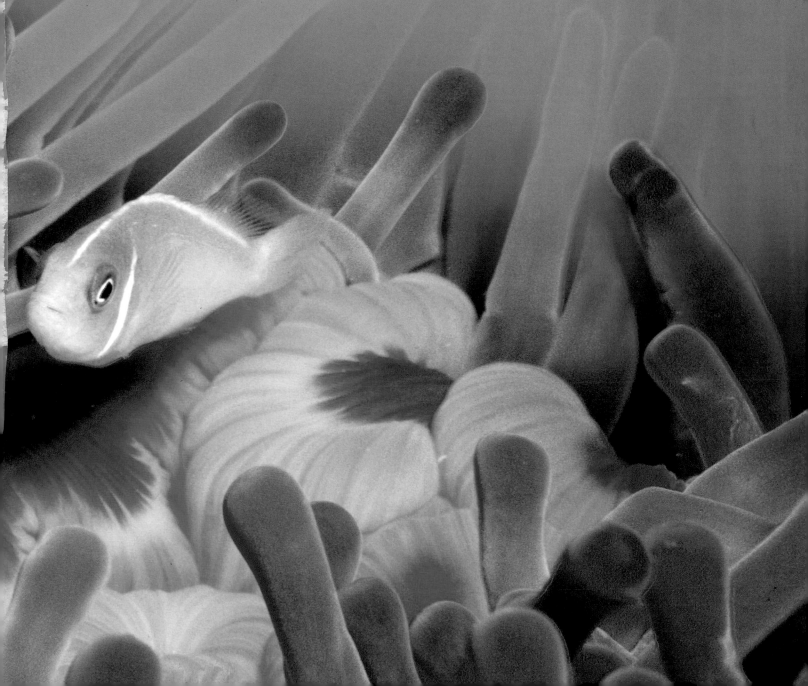

First published in 2003 by Usborne Publishing Ltd,
Usborne House, 83-85 Saffron Hill, London EC1N 8RT, England.

www.usborne.com

First published in America 2004 UE.

Printed in Italy

Usborne

INTERNET-LINKED

MYSTERIES & MARVELS
OF
NATURE

Elizabeth Dalby

Designed by Karen Tomlins, Ruth Russell,
Reuben Barrance, Michael Hill, Candice Whatmore
and Laura Hammonds

Illustrations by Candice Whatmore
and Reuben Barrance

Digital imagery by Keith Furnival
and Joanne Kirkby

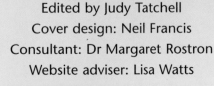

Edited by Judy Tatchell
Cover design: Neil Francis
Consultant: Dr Margaret Rostron
Website adviser: Lisa Watts

INTERNET LINKS

Throughout this book, we have suggested interesting websites where you can find out more about mysteries and marvels of nature. For example, you may be able to listen to the calls of different animals and birds, explore fascinating habitats, and find out many incredible facts and nuggets of information. To visit the sites, go to the Usborne Quicklinks Website at **www.usborne-quicklinks.com** and type the keywords "marvels of nature". There you will find links to click on to take you to all the sites.

Notes for parents

The websites described in this book are regularly reviewed and the links in Usborne Quicklinks are updated. However, the content of a website may change at any time and Usborne Publishing is not responsible for the content on any website other than its own.

We recommend that children are supervised while on the Internet, that they do not use Internet chat rooms, and that you use Internet filtering software to block unsuitable material. Please ensure that your children read and follow the safety guidelines printed on the right. For more information, see the "Net Help" area on the Usborne Quicklinks Website.

Computer not essential

If you don't have access to the Internet, don't worry. This book is a complete, self-contained book on its own.

www.usborne-quicklinks.com
Go to Usborne Quicklinks and enter the keywords "marvels of nature" for direct links to all the websites in this book.

Internet safety

When using the Internet, please make sure you follow these guidelines:
• Ask your parent's or guardian's permission before you connect to the Internet.
• If you write a message in a website guest book or on a website message board, do not include any personal information such as your full name, address or telephone number, and ask an adult before you give your email address.
• If a website asks you to log in or register by typing your name or email address, ask permission of an adult first.
• If you do receive an email from someone you don't know, tell an adult and do not reply to the email.
• Never arrange to meet anyone you have talked to on the Internet.

Site availability

The links in Usborne Quicklinks are regularly reviewed and updated, but occasionally you may get a message that a site is unavailable. This might be temporary, so try again later, or even the next day. If any of the sites close down, we will, if possible, replace them with suitable alternatives, so you will always find an up-to-date list of sites in Usborne Quicklinks.

What you need

Some websites need additional free programs, called plug-ins, to play sounds, or to show videos, animations or 3-D images. A message will appear on your screen if a site needs a particular plug-in. There is usually a button on the site that you can click on to download it. Alternatively, go to **www.usborne-quicklinks.com** and click on "Net Help". There you can find links to download plug-ins.

CONTENTS

ANIMAL-EATING PLANTS

Most plants live in soil, and get minerals and water from it. But some plants live in such poor soil that they need food from a different source as well. Though rooted to the spot, they catch live, moving animal prey.

INTERNET LINK
For a link to a website with lots of information about how Venus fly traps work and how to grow them, go to
www.usborne-quicklinks.com

Snappy trap

Venus fly traps snap shut around insects, spiders or even small frogs. Hairs on their leaves sense when something touches them. They only close around things that struggle, so don't react to things such as raindrops.

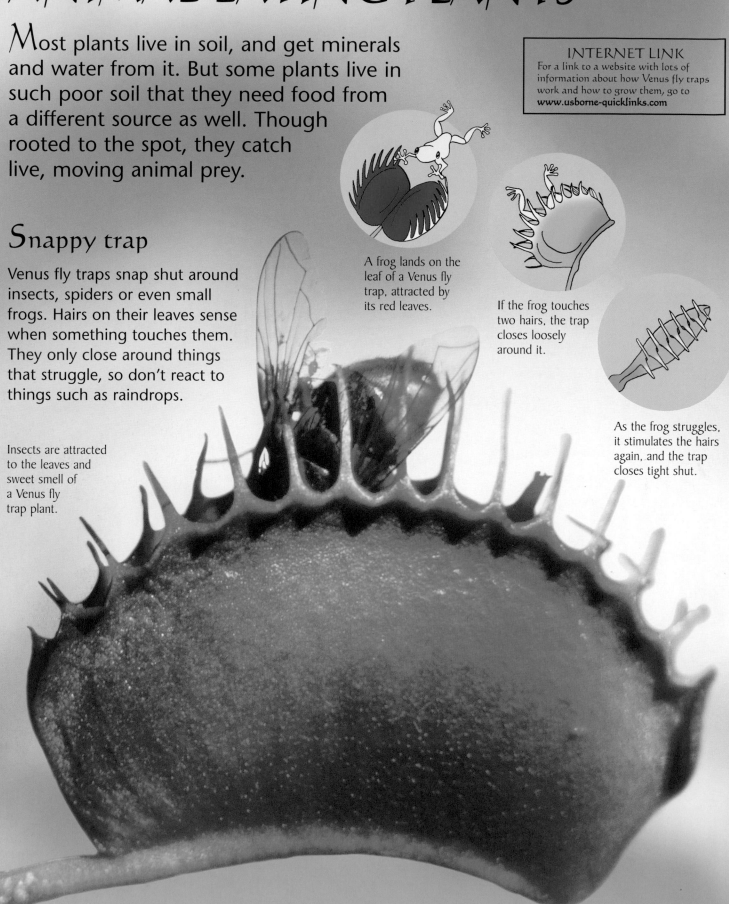

A frog lands on the leaf of a Venus fly trap, attracted by its red leaves.

If the frog touches two hairs, the trap closes loosely around it.

As the frog struggles, it stimulates the hairs again, and the trap closes tight shut.

Insects are attracted to the leaves and sweet smell of a Venus fly trap plant.

6

Slippery slope

Pitcher plants lure insects to their death by producing strong-smelling nectar. Insects go into the pitcher looking for the nectar, and fall into a mixture of water and digestive juices at the bottom. The insect's body is broken down and dissolved in this liquid, so the plant can absorb the nutrients from it.

Hood

An insect is attracted to a pitcher by the nectar produced by a gland near its hood.

Downward-pointing hairs line the pitcher's tube. The insect easily slips and tumbles in.

The pitcher hangs on a tendril that grows on the end of a leaf.

Stuck fast

Insects that are attracted to the shiny, red-tipped tentacles that cover a sundew's leaf get a nasty surprise. Instead of finding a meal of nectar, the insect becomes a meal for the sundew.

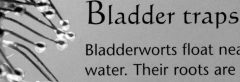

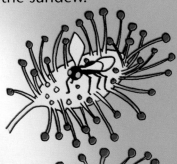

An insect lands on the sundew's leaf, and gets stuck to the sticky, sweet-smelling tentacles.

The tentacles release fluids that begin to digest the insect. The leaf slowly curls around the insect.

When the leaf opens again, the insect is completely digested. Only its hard outer case is left behind.

Bladder traps

Bladderworts float near the surface of water. Their roots are tipped by hundreds of tiny traps, called bladders.

A small creature, such as a water flea, swims past a bladder and touches sensitive hairs.

The bladder expands, and its door opens. Water rushes in, and the creature is sucked in too.

The door shuts, trapping the creature inside the bladder, where it will be digested.

OCEAN FEEDING

Some ocean creatures, such as great white sharks, use sheer force to catch their prey. Others use cunning, encouraging small creatures to swim straight into the jaws of death.

A great white shark strikes with such speed and force that its first bite usually kills its prey.

Unfussy eater

The great white shark is one of the most terrifying creatures in the sea. It has fearsome teeth and a powerful body. It feeds on dolphins, porpoises and fish, even other sharks. Most of all it likes to eat seals and sea lions.

The shark uses its first two rows of teeth. The back rows move up when these wear out and more will grow behind. Some sharks go through 50,000 teeth in their lifetime.

A great white shark's teeth have jagged edges to saw through flesh. A shark may have up to 3,000 teeth in its mouth at any one time.

Bubble net fishing

Humpback whales work as a team to catch fish. They round up a school of fish using streams of bubbles as nets. Then each whale expands its throat and belly, and sucks in vast amounts of water containing lots of fish.

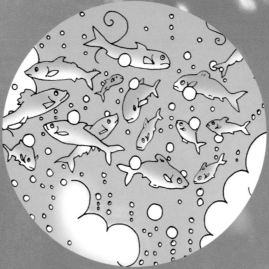

The fish become confused by the "net" of bubbles, and seem unable to swim away.

The whales swim up through the school of fish, mouths wide open, gulping down hundreds of fish. Then they filter the water out of their mouths, leaving only the fish inside.

A group of whales sinks below a school of herrings. Each whale releases streams of bubbles.

INTERNET LINK
For a link to a website where you can find out more about the fascinating feeding habits of frogfish, go to www.usborne-quicklinks.com

Starfish stealth

Shellfish with hinged shells are called bivalves. Their shells protect them from many enemies, but not from the harmless-looking starfish. These have powerful suckers on their arms, and an excellent sense of smell. When they sniff out a bivalve, they use their suckers to pull its shell open and get at its soft body.

A starfish grips a shellfish with its suckered arms and forces the shell open. It digests the shellfish inside by slipping its own stomach right into the shell.

Suction surprise

Frogfish crawl around coral reefs on their fins. Their rough skin helps them blend into the background. Sometimes the only visible part of a frogfish is its rod-like lure, which grows from a spine on its back and dangles in front of its mouth. The lure tricks other fish into coming closer.

The frogfish hides among coral and wiggles its lure. The lure may look like a small fish, or have a light on it, like this one.

Another fish swims closer to take a look. As it comes near, the frogfish suddenly opens its mouth to 12 times its normal size.

As water rushes into the frogfish's mouth, the other fish is sucked inside. This all happens in only a 6,000th of a second.

CATCHING DINNER

Reptiles, such as snakes and crocodiles, can survive for weeks, or even months, without food. Many eat huge meals when they get the chance, though. They use all their senses, skill and cunning to catch their prey.

Aerial ambush

Eyelash vipers lurk in rainforest trees, waiting for their prey. Their green, brown or yellow markings help them hide among the leaves and flowers. They can survive for up to a year between meals, but when a frog, bird or small rodent comes near, the viper strikes. It poisons the creature, then eats it.

Snapped up

An alligator snapping turtle is hiding at the bottom of a muddy swamp. Its shell is almost invisible.

The turtle has a piece of pink skin in its mouth, called a lure, which looks like a worm. It wiggles this to attract fish.

Any creature that comes to investigate the turtle's lure may be snapped up. It only takes a split second.

An eyelash viper uses its tail to grip a branch while it catches and eats its prey.

Tongue tactics

Chameleons feed on insects, frogs and small reptiles. They use their sharp eyesight to pinpoint prey. A chameleon's secret weapon is its tongue, which can extend longer than its body. The tongue forms a suction cup at the end, which sticks to the prey. It snaps back into the chameleon's mouth like elastic.

An eyelash viper is small but it can swallow prey larger than its own head. It does this by unhinging its upper and lower jaws so they can stretch apart.

A chameleon's tongue is a hollow tube that fits around a bone inside its mouth.

When muscles in the tongue pull tight around the bone, the tongue becomes very long and thin, and shoots out.

A chameleon's toes are designed for gripping branches. It also uses its tail to hang on.

Poison flows through the middle of an eyelash viper's hollow fangs. The long fangs fold back when the snake's mouth is closed.

INTERNET LINK
For a link to a website where you can find out more about what snakes like to eat, go to www.usborne-quicklinks.com

Surprise snack

A Nile crocodile will eat almost anything that comes its way, such as fishes, turtles and frogs. It can even kill large animals such as wildebeest that come to the river to drink. It lurks at the water's edge and attacks with astonishing speed. It grabs the victim in its powerful jaws and drags it into the water to drown.

A crocodile lurks silently in the water, with only its eyes poking above the surface.

With one snap of its fearsome jaws, the crocodile grips its prey.

The crocodile lifts its head and tips it back before swallowing, to avoid taking in a lot of water.

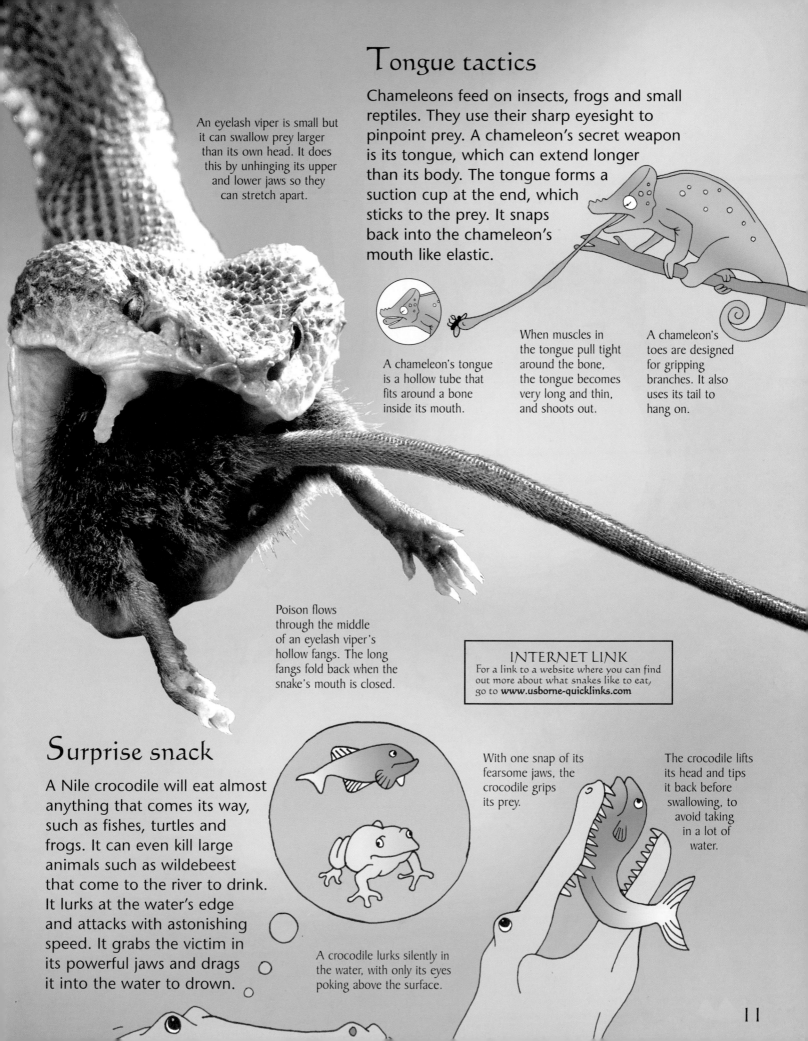

FOOD ON THE MOVE

Birds catch food using only their beaks or their feet. They must strike quickly, or go hungry. Some use speed, aerobatic skills and keen eyesight to catch prey. Others use stealth, cunning and even bait, to lure their prey within striking distance.

Fly fishing

Kingfishers are small but spectacular hunters. They catch insects in mid-air and dive into rivers to catch fish. A kingfisher dives so fast that it looks like a brilliant blue streak. Its beak is exactly the right shape to snatch a slippery fish from the water.

INTERNET LINK
For a link to a website where you can see photographs of pelicans fishing as a team, go to www.usborne-quicklinks.com

A kingfisher scans the water for fish, from a perch or while hovering. If it sees a fish, it goes into a dive.

It dives at an angle of 45°, making quick wingbeats to speed itself as it nears the surface of the water.

The kingfisher closes its eyes as it hits the water, and grabs the fish in its beak. It swallows it whole.

Group fishing

A pelican has a large beak with a stretchy pouch to hold a big catch of fish. Instead of fishing alone, pelicans work in teams. This gives each pelican a better chance of a good meal.

This brown pelican's pouch is stretched out of shape by the big fish it has caught.

The pelicans herd fish ahead of them into shallow water, by flapping their wings.

When the fish are in shallow water, the pelicans scoop them up in their huge beaks.

A pelican tips its beak down to let water run out before tipping it back to swallow.

Wait or bait

A green heron stands like a statue at the edge of the water, waiting for an unwary fish to swim by. If a fish does arrive, the heron attacks swiftly. If no fish comes along, the heron will try to attract one using bait.

A heron places its bait. This may be an insect or a small object like a feather.

Fish nearby are interested in the bait and come to take a closer look.

The heron strikes like lightning, spearing the fish on the end of its pointed beak.

Terrible talons

Owls have long claws, called talons, designed to kill. An owl tears its food apart with its beak and talons, or swallows small animals whole. Later, it spits out any body parts that it can't digest, such as bones or fur, in the form of a pellet.

Super senses

Owls hunt at night. They have super-keen hearing that can pick up the rustle of a mouse moving on the ground, from the top of a tall tree. An owl's ears are on the sides of its head, but face to the front. In the picture above, you can see two dish shapes on the owl's face which help to channel sounds into its ears.

This mouse is carrying a berry for its own meal. It hasn't heard the owl swooping down on it.

MAMMALS' MEALS

If an animal doesn't eat, it dies. Stealth and speed are the secret weapons of many hungry mammals. These are animals that have hair on their bodies and feed their babies with milk. Some use special tools, such as a long tongue or claw, to find food.

Vampire bats hunt at night.

Hidden treats

An aye-aye's special tool is its long, bony middle finger, tipped with a curved claw. It taps on a tree, listening for the hollow sounds of insects' tunnels. It then chews away the bark and probes for its prey.

Aerial anteater

Tamanduas are anteaters that live in trees. They eat ants, termites, bees and honey. They have a clever way of making sure their food supply doesn't run out.

A tamandua rips open a nest of insects with its claws. It uses its tongue to lick up the occupants.

It doesn't entirely destroy the nest, though. It lets some insects survive so they can rebuild the nest and colony.

This means that the tamandua can come back later for another feast of insects from the same nest.

An aye-aye uses its long, bony middle finger to scoop insects and grubs out of the hole it has made.

14

Blood lappers

Vampire bats are the only mammals that feed on other animals' blood. A bat needs to eat at least every two nights to survive and may spend two hours feeding from a single animal. It bites a hole in the animal's skin with its long, sharp front teeth. The hole fills with blood, which the bat laps up.

Vampire bats use hearing and smell to find sleeping animals to feed from.

Tall order

Giraffes are designed to reach the parts of trees that other animals – apart from elephants – can't. With their extra-long necks and legs, giraffes feed on the juicy leaves of acacia and mimosa trees. They need to feed for up to 20 hours every day.

A giraffe's tongue can be over 50cm (20in) long – even longer than an anteater's.

The giraffe can grab leaves with its rubbery upper lip. But if the tree is thorny, it uses its long tongue to pluck leaves from between the thorns.

INTERNET LINK
For a link to a website where you can find lots of interesting vampire bat facts, go to www.usborne-quicklinks.com

Surprise attack

To catch food, tigers use stealth. A tiger tracks down its prey (deer, wild pigs and rodents), using its excellent vision, hearing and sense of smell. It then takes its time moving quietly into an attacking position. When it is within 25m (80ft) of its victim, it charges.

A tiger can easily leap up to 6m (20ft). To kill its prey, it bites the back of an animal's neck, or its throat.

FEEDING FEATURES

Insects and spiders have specially designed bodies to cope with the kind of food they eat. They also have clever ways of catching their prey.

Sticky situation

The silk that spiders use to spin their webs is extremely thin and very stretchy. Some of this silk is smooth, for the spider to walk on. Some is sticky, to trap passing insects. The silk is made in glands called spinnerets. It leaves the spider's body as a liquid that hardens in the air.

An orange orb spider lies in wait on its web in the Amazon rainforest.

A spider starts its web by spinning the first thread into the air. The wind carries it to a second point, where it sticks. The spider carefully walks across this thread.

The spider walks back and forth along the thread, making it thicker. It then spins a second thread to make a "Y" shape. Gradually, it adds more threads from the central point.

The web now looks like the spokes of a bicycle wheel. The spider spirals around the spokes, spinning more silk as it goes, to complete the web.

Some orb spiders make a new web every day. Before they make a new web, they eat the old one, to avoid wasting the protein that makes up the silk.

Spider silk is five times stronger than steel wire would be – if steel wire could be made as thin.

Eating out

There are around six million different kinds of insects. They eat a huge variety of food, from flower nectar and plant juices to dead animals.

Insects' mouthparts are designed to cope with their different diets.

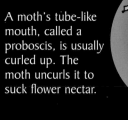

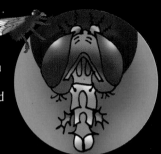

A moth's tube-like mouth, called a proboscis, is usually curled up. The moth uncurls it to suck flower nectar.

The long, tube-like part of a cicada's mouth drills into plants. It can then suck up the juices inside.

A housefly's mouthparts have a sponge-like end. This mops up food softened by the fly's saliva.

Beetles have mouthparts that can bite and chew. They feed mainly on dead plants or animals.

Fungus farmers

Leaf-cutter ants grow their own food. They strip leaves from nearby trees, cut the leaves into pieces and carry them back to their underground nest. There, other ants bite the pieces of leaf into smaller pieces and mix them with saliva. A kind of fungus grows on this leaf mixture, and it's this fungus that the ants eat.

This small ant's job is to defend the larger ant from a type of fly that attacks ants while they are carrying leaves and unable to defend themselves.

A colony of leaf-cutter ants can strip a tree of leaves in a single day.

This ant is carrying a piece of leaf back to the nest. The leaf may be two or three times as heavy as the ant.

INTERNET LINK
For a link to a website where you can find out about the techniques different kinds of spiders use to catch their prey, go to
www.usborne-quicklinks.com

17

PLANTS ON THE MOVE

It might be hard to believe that plants move – but most can move parts of themselves, a little. Many grow or move in the direction of things they need, such as sunlight or water.

Dandelion seeds are designed to move on the wind, so that they can be carried to new homes.

Sun lover

For a plant to bend, turn its head or grow in a different direction, the cells in the affected part have to change shape. Plant movements like this are called tropisms. Some tropisms, such as the one below, might happen in minutes.

As the Sun rises, the stem of a sunflower bends so the flower head faces the Sun.

Cells in the side of the stem facing away from the Sun expand to make this happen.

The sunflowers follow the Sun's movement across the sky. This is called heliotropism.

This vine grows tendrils from its stem or leaves. When it touches something, the tendril curls around it for support.

This is a passionflower vine. It can grow to over 9m (30ft) long.

Cunning creeper

Vines have roots in the ground but cling to other plants for support. They grow as fast as they can in the direction of the most sunlight. Because they don't support themselves, they can put all their energy into growing longer.

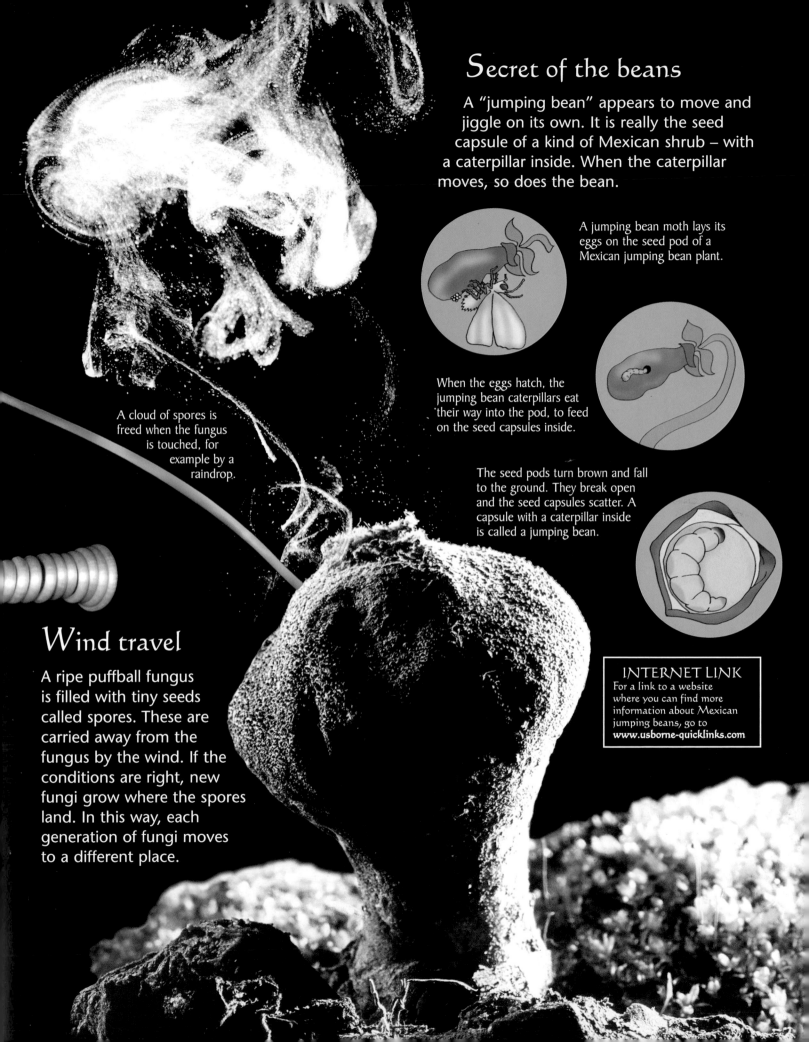

Secret of the beans

A "jumping bean" appears to move and jiggle on its own. It is really the seed capsule of a kind of Mexican shrub – with a caterpillar inside. When the caterpillar moves, so does the bean.

A jumping bean moth lays its eggs on the seed pod of a Mexican jumping bean plant.

When the eggs hatch, the jumping bean caterpillars eat their way into the pod, to feed on the seed capsules inside.

The seed pods turn brown and fall to the ground. They break open and the seed capsules scatter. A capsule with a caterpillar inside is called a jumping bean.

A cloud of spores is freed when the fungus is touched, for example by a raindrop.

INTERNET LINK
For a link to a website where you can find more information about Mexican jumping beans, go to
www.usborne-quicklinks.com

Wind travel

A ripe puffball fungus is filled with tiny seeds called spores. These are carried away from the fungus by the wind. If the conditions are right, new fungi grow where the spores land. In this way, each generation of fungi moves to a different place.

MOVING THROUGH WATER

Not everything that lives in the ocean swims like a fish. There are lots of other ways of moving through the water, including hitching a ride.

This remora has stuck itself to the underside of a turtle. The faster the turtle swims, the tighter the remora grips.

Sucker fish

A remora is a fish with a sucker near the top of its head. It can attach this sucker to a shark, ray, turtle or even a boat. It is pulled through the water and feeds on scraps of food dropped by its host. It finds more food this way than it would on its own.

A remora has a ridged sucker. When the ridges are raised against a surface, they grip very strongly.

Helpful passenger

Sea anemones usually attach themselves to rock or coral. They catch food in their tentacles. One way to get a ride to a different place where there might be more food, is to hitch a lift with a hermit crab.

This hermit crab has three sea anemones attached to it. They feed on scraps of food dropped by the crab.

Sea anemones
Crab's body and legs
Crab's eyes
Crab's shell

Sea anemones protect the crab. They are poisonous and also help to hide it.

Super swimmer

A squid can move very fast in any direction, using jet propulsion. Its fins act as stabilizers. It also uses its fins to swim more slowly. A squid can swim for long periods of time over great distances in its search for food. It starts off with jet propulsion, then switches to fin-power.

A squid's body is supported inside by a stiff rod called a pen, made of a substance called chitin.

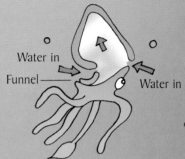

Water in

Funnel

Water in

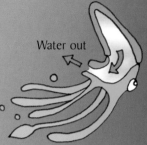

Water out

The squid takes water into its strong, muscular body. It angles its funnel, ready to move.

It squeezes water out through its funnel. This jet-propels it in the opposite direction.

INTERNET LINK
For a link to a website where you can find out more about the amazing remora, go to www.usborne-quicklinks.com

Speed or steer?

Fish are specially designed to cope with moving through water, which is denser than air. Some are built for speed, but can't rapidly change direction. Others don't move fast, but are able to twist and turn between rocks, reefs and plants.

Eels use their back and underside fins to move. They are able to back their long bodies into narrow caves.

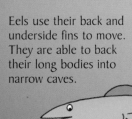

Parrotfish use their side fins to paddle. They can twist and turn easily, weaving between coral reefs.

Sharks use their tail fins to propel themselves. They can move very fast but are unable to turn quickly or swim in reverse.

21

GLIDING AND SLIDING

Reptiles and amphibians, such as snakes, lizards and frogs, move in a variety of ways. Some can even travel across the surface of water or soft, shifting sands. Others, like the tree frog on the right, can glide through the air.

This tree frog is 1/3 actual size.

Moving around can take a long time for a small animal in a rainforest. A Wallace's tree frog saves time by gliding up to 15m (50ft) between trees.

Sideways motion

Sidewinders get their name from the way they move. They live in sandy deserts where the surface is scorching hot and slippery. The sidewinder moves by looping its body sideways, which helps it get a grip on the surface of the sand. It also means that less of its body touches the hot sand at any time.

The frog's toes are very long, and webbing between them acts like a sail or parachute. Pads on its toes grip firmly when it lands.

As it throws its body sideways, a sidewinder leaves distinctive tracks in the desert sand.

Tail talents

Crested geckos jump between trees to get around in the rainforest. A gecko uses its grasping tail like a fifth limb to cling onto branches, or like a rudder to help it balance and steer in the air.

INTERNET LINK
For a link to a website where you can find out more about the secret of a gecko's sticky feet, go to **www.usborne-quicklinks.com**

The underside of each foot is covered in two million hairs.

Sticky feet

Geckos are able to walk on vertical surfaces and even upside-down, as if their feet were covered in glue. In fact, each foot is covered in millions of tiny hairs, which bond with surfaces to help the gecko cling on.

There are tiny forces of electrical attraction between the hairs on a gecko's foot and the surfaces it walks on. This makes them stick together.

No time to sink

Basilisk lizards can walk on water. This is possible because they are light, with large, fringed feet. They move too fast to sink. If a lizard can't escape on the surface of the water, it may let itself sink and try swimming to safety instead.

Basilisk lizards can run at speeds of up to 12kph (7.5mph) – about twice as fast as a person walking quickly.

AIR, LAND AND WATER

All birds have wings but not all birds are able, or choose, to fly. Some prefer to walk or swim, for instance. Birds that do fly have different ways of taking off and staying up in the air.

Lift-off

The bigger the bird, the bigger the wingspan it needs to achieve lift-off.

Swans are among the largest waterbirds. As well as big wings, they need a running start of up to 40m (130ft), before they can take off. They run into the wind, to speed up the flow of air over their wings. This helps lift them into the air.

A swan runs across the surface of the water on its large, webbed feet, getting up speed for take-off.

INTERNET LINK
For a link to a website where you can find out more about how birds are able to fly, go to
www.usborne-quicklinks.com

Aerial agility

Tiny hummingbirds depend on their agility in the air to outwit large predators such as hawks. Their wings beat up to 90 times each second. A hummingbird can fly in any direction and can even hover in mid-air. They rarely walk along the ground, but they do perch briefly on branches or on the ground in between flights.

Hummingbirds need a lot of energy to maintain their high-speed life. They feed almost constantly on sugary flower nectar.

Water walker

African jacanas are quite heavy birds but they are able to run across the surface of water, supported only by delicate plants such as water lilies. They can do this because they have incredibly long toes, which spread their weight across a large area. They don't often walk on land – their long toes make this difficult. But they can fly, and they are excellent swimmers and divers.

Water plants help support a jacana as it skips across the surface.

Compared to its body size, the African jacana has the largest toes of any bird.

Speed swimming

Chinstrap penguins waddle awkwardly on their feet over the ice. On snow they find it easier, and quicker, to "toboggan" on their chests, pushing themselves along with their wings. They are most agile in the water. They can swim fast enough to outpace leopard seals, and can leap out of the water onto ice floes up to 2m (6.5ft) high.

Chinstrap penguins use their feet as powerful paddles in the water. Their wings act as flippers when they are swimming, to help them steer.

MADE TO MOVE

Mammals have developed some amazing ways of getting from one place to another, both on the ground and in the air.

Jumping power

Kangaroos are shy and usually stay hidden during the day. But at night, they leap across the Australian landscape, looking for fresh grass to eat. They can reach speeds of up to 48kph (30mph) – and amazingly, the faster they go, the less energy they use up.

This is possible because when it is jumping, a kangaroo's legs act like springs. The energy from the first jump stays in the kangaroo's legs and is used to power the next jump. This jump then helps to power the next, and so on.

A kangaroo stretches its tail out behind when it jumps, to help it balance.

Kangaroos can jump up to 3m (10ft) high.

Kangaroos' legs are very well-suited to jumping but this means that they can't walk very well.

INTERNET LINK
For a link to a website where you can find information about how different mammals move around, go to www.usborne-quicklinks.com

Hidden wings

A sugar glider conceals a secret method of movement. Two flaps of skin between its front and back legs can be stretched to form "wings" called gliding membranes. The sugar glider uses the membranes to parachute from one tree to another, in its search for insects, nectar and sap to eat.

When a sugar glider is resting, the skin flaps are barely visible.

When it is in the air, the skin flaps stretch. Muscles in them let the glider steer.

Born to run

A cheetah has a long stride, made possible by its very flexible spine. As it reaches out with its front legs, the spine curves down.

As the front legs push back, the spine curves up. This lets the back legs come all the way forward, ready to push off again.

Cheetahs are the fastest animals on land, with a top speed of 115kph (70mph). Every part of a cheetah's streamlined body is designed for speed. It has large paw pads and claws to grip the ground firmly. Its skeleton is strong and very light. Its extra-large nostrils and lungs can take in lots of oxygen when the cheetah is running.

Kangaroos have sharp claws on their small front paws, for fighting.

Red kangaroos are the largest marsupials – these are mammals with pouches for their young.

A kangaroo can travel up to 9m (30ft) in one bound.

WINGS AND LEGS

Some insects are capable of truly amazing feats of flight, from displays of speed and agility to incredible endurance. Other small creatures can make great leaps to catch prey – or to avoid being caught themselves.

Monarch migration

Every winter, millions of monarch butterflies leave their homes in North America and travel south to Mexico where the weather is warmer. The following summer, they return north to breed.

This kind of return trip, to find warmer weather, is called a migration. Many other butterflies spend the winter as eggs or larvae. They emerge as adults in spring.

Monarch butterflies stop to drink nectar to fuel their journey. To save energy, they try to glide as much as possible.

The red lines show some of the monarchs' routes from North America to Mexico – up to 4,800km (3,000 miles).

Jumping spiders have good eyesight so they hit their target.

Long leap

Jumping spiders can jump 50 times the length of their own bodies to catch prey. They don't have very big leg muscles, though. Instead, a spider jumps by lifting up its front legs and then contracting the muscles in its body. This raises its blood pressure, which forces fluid into the back legs. They straighten very quickly, propelling the spider into the air.

Fantastic fliers

Dragonflies are among the fastest flying insects. They can reach speeds of up to 95kph (60mph). They can also hover – useful while they seek out prey with their sharp eyes – and can dart in different directions. They do all this in spite of having a primitive wing design that has not changed for millions of years.

A dragonfly's body is tilted so that its legs hang below its jaws. Here, it is about to catch a mosquito in its basket of legs.

It eats the mosquito as it flies, with its strong, biting mouthparts.

Dragonflies have two pairs of wings. The front pair can move independently of the back pair.

INTERNET LINK
For a link to a website where you can find out more about jumping spiders, go to www.usborne-quicklinks.com

Muscle power

Grasshoppers have several ways of moving. Like most insects, they have six legs and two pairs of wings, and can crawl or fly. They also have very long, muscular back legs, which let them make incredible jumps. If a grasshopper were the size of a person, it would be able to jump 40m (130ft) from a standstill.

Preparing to jump, the grasshopper crouches, with its back legs folded.

The leg muscles contract and the legs straighten, launching the grasshopper.

29

PLANTS FIGHT BACK

Plants can't run away from their enemies but many defend themselves fiercely. Some even produce poisons that can kill animals that try to eat them.

Thorny issue

Umbrella thorn acacias are the most common trees on the African grasslands. Grazing animals would devour their juicy leaves, if they weren't protected by thorns. The acacias have two different kinds of thorns – long, straight, white thorns and small, brown, hooked thorns. Each kind of thorn puts off different animals.

An acacia's thorns are arranged in clusters.

The only animal with a mouth tough enough to deal with the acacia's thorns is a giraffe.

Fearsome fungi

Some mushrooms are armed with deadly poisons. The most poisonous mushroom in the world is the death cap. People sometimes mistake this for an edible mushroom, with fatal results. A relative of the death cap is the poisonous fly agaric, shown in the photograph. Every part of this mushroom is poisonous, even its spores. Its bright cap is easy to recognize, though.

The white scales on this fly agaric's cap and the frill on its stalk are leftovers from the covering it had when it was growing.

Death caps can be difficult to identify. They may look like some types of edible mushrooms.

Prickly protection

Cactus spines put off most grazing animals. Prickly pear cacti, like the one in this photo, have two kinds of spines – large, widely-spaced spikes, and clumps of tiny spines which irritate if they get under skin. Some animals, such as iguanas, have mouths tough enough to eat the cacti anyway. Rabbits, also, are able to nibble the juicy flesh between the spines.

Many cacti grow in deserts. Desert animals eat them because they are moist and full of nutrients.

Some birds build their nests inside the stems of cacti. The spines give them protection from predators.

Bolshy bush

Creosote bushes are very successful desert plants. Their waxy leaves help to stop them from losing too much water. The leaves also taste terrible to grazing animals. The bushes compete against other desert plants by giving off poisons from their roots. This prevents other plants from growing too near and taking valuable water.

The oldest-known creosote bush is 9,400 years old.

New shoots grow up around the outside of a creosote bush. Eventually the middle part dies, leaving a ring of new growth, which is all part of the original plant.

The prickly pear's large spines keep most animals at a distance.

The small spines, called glochids, break off easily if they are touched.

INTERNET LINK
For a link to a website where you can browse a list of poisonous plants, go to www.usborne-quicklinks.com

WATER WEAPONS

Some ocean creatures are able to attack and kill much faster, stronger animals, or defend themselves against animals several times their own size. Many use deadly stings or even electric shocks.

Terrible tentacles

Jellyfish have tentacles which they use to catch small fish or other creatures to eat. The tentacles are covered in stinging cells. These deliver powerful poison to the victims which are usually killed or paralyzed immediately. The jellyfish has "arms" which move food caught by its tentacles to its mouth, in the middle of its body.

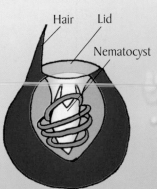

Hair   Lid

Nematocyst

A stinging cell consists of a sensitive hair, a lid, and a nematocyst, which fires like a miniature harpoon if the hair is touched.

This is a sea nettle jellyfish. When its tentacles sting, they also stick tight to the victim, trapping it completely.

INTERNET LINK
For a link to a website where you can find more information about different kinds of jellyfish, go to
www.usborne-quicklinks.com

Small but deadly

A blue-ringed octopus is only the size of a golfball but it is one of the most poisonous creatures in the sea. It contains enough poison to kill 25 men, and there is no known antidote. Because it is so small, it can be difficult to spot before it's too late.

A blue-ringed octopus usually blends into the sand and rocks on the bottom of the sea.

If it is agitated, for example if it is about to attack, it turns bright yellow with blue ring markings.

Final attack

Porcupine fish defend themselves against enemies by taking water into their stomachs and inflating to twice their normal size. They can even inflate in a predator's throat, if they have already been swallowed. This doesn't save the porcupine fish, but it does kill its predator as well.

A porcupine fish's spines usually lie flat. As it inflates, they stick out and this scares many attackers off. An inflated fish can't swim fast, so it just hopes its attacker will give up.

Shock tactics

Torpedo rays use electric shocks to stun fish and shellfish. They have two electrical organs near their heads that work like batteries. These can give electric shocks powerful enough to kill a fish – but not a person.

A torpedo ray has electrical organs near its head. They make up about one-sixth of its total body weight.

POISONING AND SQUEEZING

Many snakes use poison, called venom, to attack or to defend themselves. They bite their enemies. Other snakes squeeze their victims to death. Some rainforest frogs have poisonous skins to protect themselves.

This is a strawberry poison dart frog. Its bright markings warn predators to stay away, because its skin is covered with a poisonous slime.

This frog lives in the South American rainforest.

Poisoned skin

Poison dart frogs have moist skin that is covered in a poisonous slime. Some rainforest people coat the tips of blow-gun darts with this poison and use them for hunting small animals. One frog may produce enough poison to coat the tips of 50 darts.

Spitting snake

If it is threatened, a spitting cobra can shoot a spray of poison, or venom, at the eyes of an enemy. It can hit its target up to 2m (7ft) away. The venom causes temporary blindness, so the snake can dart in and deliver a poisonous bite. It's the bite that actually kills the enemy.

Muscles contract and pump venom from a sac through holes in the cobra's fangs.

The snake breathes air out. This passes through the venom, making a spray.

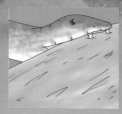

The spray blinds the victim. The cobra then attacks with its teeth, injecting more venom.

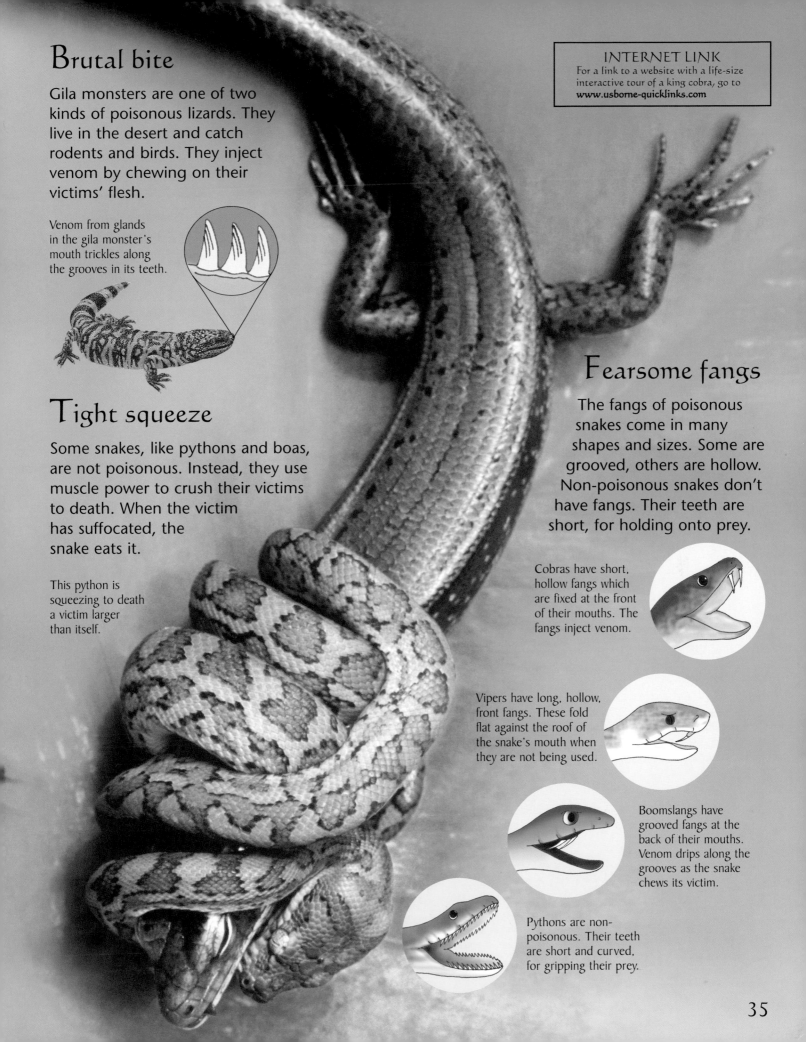

Brutal bite

Gila monsters are one of two kinds of poisonous lizards. They live in the desert and catch rodents and birds. They inject venom by chewing on their victims' flesh.

Venom from glands in the gila monster's mouth trickles along the grooves in its teeth.

Tight squeeze

Some snakes, like pythons and boas, are not poisonous. Instead, they use muscle power to crush their victims to death. When the victim has suffocated, the snake eats it.

This python is squeezing to death a victim larger than itself.

INTERNET LINK
For a link to a website with a life-size interactive tour of a king cobra, go to www.usborne-quicklinks.com

Fearsome fangs

The fangs of poisonous snakes come in many shapes and sizes. Some are grooved, others are hollow. Non-poisonous snakes don't have fangs. Their teeth are short, for holding onto prey.

Cobras have short, hollow fangs which are fixed at the front of their mouths. The fangs inject venom.

Vipers have long, hollow, front fangs. These fold flat against the roof of the snake's mouth when they are not being used.

Boomslangs have grooved fangs at the back of their mouths. Venom drips along the grooves as the snake chews its victim.

Pythons are non-poisonous. Their teeth are short and curved, for gripping their prey.

35

BIRD BATTLES

Most birds defend the areas where they breed or feed. These areas are called territories. Disputes over territories can end in dramatic and vicious fighting – or even death.

Although snowy egrets have long, sharp beaks and fight often, they don't usually injure each other.

Beak wrestling

Male snowy egrets defend quite large territories. A bird performs displays in its own territory to keep other males away and also to attract females. When two male egrets fight, they wrestle with their beaks. This helps them decide which bird is the stronger, without either getting badly injured.

Territorial tapping

Male woodpeckers use sound to communicate with rival males and to attract females. Instead of singing, they tap out messages with their beaks on the bark of trees. Woodpeckers learn to recognize the different rhythms made by other birds, telling them to stay away or inviting them closer.

To make a loud tap, a woodpecker hits the tree hard with its beak.

The woodpecker also uses its beak to scoop insects out of tree bark.

It lives in a nest, carved with its beak out of a tree trunk.

Fighting for fish

Going into battle against a bald eagle, with its fearsome beak and talons, is a risky thing to do – even for another bald eagle. But sometimes they do fight among themselves, to claim territory or just to steal a rival's fish. Fights over territory sometimes end in death for the losing eagle.

Bald eagles sometimes use their sharp beaks and talons against each other, to steal food.

INTERNET LINK
For a link to a website with more about bald eagles, go to www.usborne-quicklinks.com

Safety in numbers

Gannets nest in huge colonies of thousands of birds but they only do so because it gives greater protection from enemies. They are not really sociable or cooperative. They share their feeding territory but each bird fiercely defends its own tiny breeding territory. It will attack other bird or animal intruders.

Warning song

Male European robins are fierce defenders of their territory. They will viciously attack any intruders, especially at nesting time. Robins sing songs to warn off other males. This means they don't need to patrol their territory all the time.

A robin's red breast gives him away if he dares to enter a rival male's territory.

A gannet defends its tiny breeding territory against another gannet. It attacks the intruder with its sharp beak to scare it away.

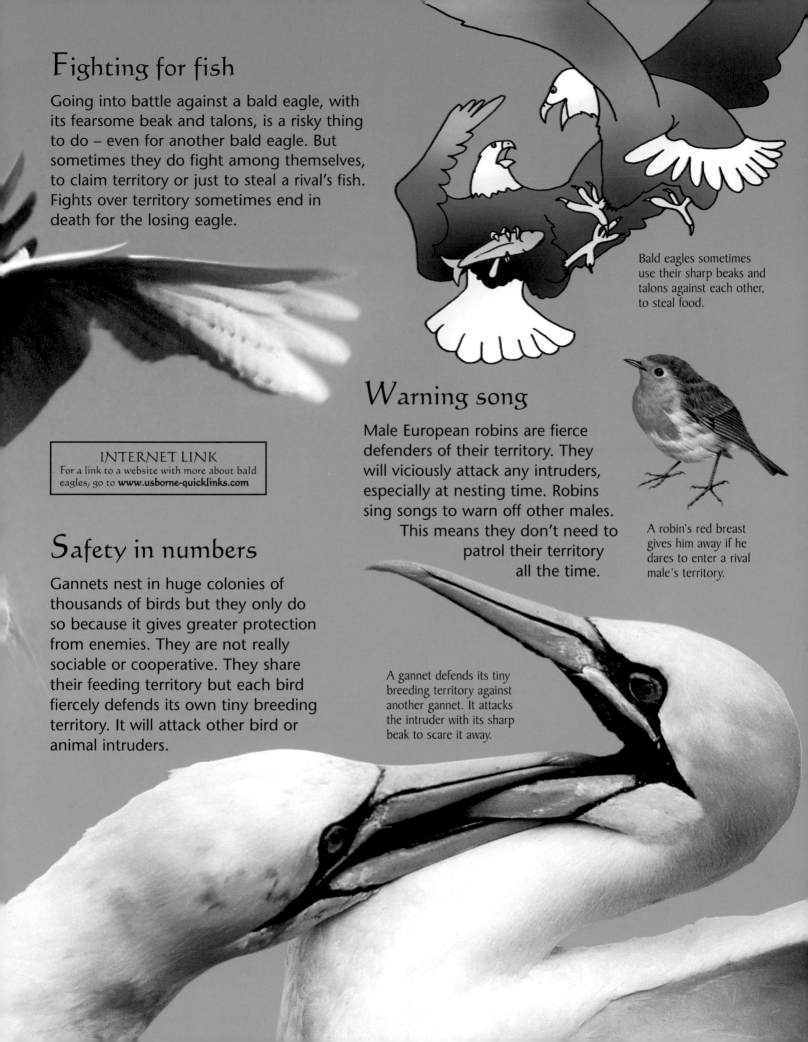

TAKE ME ON

Many mammals fight among themselves, trying to impress a mate. Some of their contests turn into spectacular displays of physical strength and superiority – sometimes ending in death.

The fighting life

Wolves live in groups called packs. Both males and females fight to decide who is top wolf of the pack. The top male and female mate with each other. Wolves from different packs fight when they meet, and some wolves may be killed.

These wolves from the same pack are play-fighting. They do this from an early age, preparing for real fights.

INTERNET LINK
For a link to a website with information about the "wolf within" and pack mentality, go to **www.usborne-quicklinks.com**

Poisonous platypus

The duck-billed platypus is one of only three poisonous mammals. The males have horn-like spurs on their back legs. These spurs are hollow and are connected to a poison gland. The poison is strong enough to kill small animals. Scientists think that platypuses use their spurs to fight with rival males over females or territory.

A platypus has webbed feet for swimming. Only the back legs have spurs.

Brand new headgear

Every year, a bull moose grows a new set of antlers. This takes a lot of energy and the moose needs extra minerals. It gets these by eating willow shoots, bones and even old antlers. Usually the moose with the biggest antlers gets the most females – the males rarely fight with their antlers. This avoids unnecessary injury.

At the start of the summer, a bull moose's antlers are just small, velvety knobs. They grow quickly – about 1cm (0.5in), or 0.5kg (1lb), every day.

The velvety skin on the growing antlers supplies them with blood and minerals. When the antlers are fully grown, the moose rubs the velvet off against trees and rocks.

Antlers are made of bone. A bull moose's antlers may span 1.8m (6ft) and weigh as much as 36kg (80lbs). At the end of the summer, the antlers drop off.

Triumphant tusks

Walrus tusks have several uses. They are good for making holes in the Arctic ice, and they help a walrus to pull itself out of the sea when it returns to land. They also help male walruses to decide which is the most dominant – the bigger the tusks, the more important the walrus.

Only walruses with similar-sized tusks fight, to decide which is superior.

A walrus's tusks are enlarged front teeth. They may be up to 90cm (3ft) long.

INSECT ATTACK

Insects are able to attack enemies much larger than themselves. Many use chemical warfare, such as poisons and burning liquids, to defend themselves or catch prey.

Lurking lion

The larvae of some kinds of lacewings are called ant-lions, because they prey ferociously on ants. Ant-lions live in sandy areas. They dig cone-shaped traps to catch their prey.

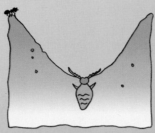

An ant-lion buries itself almost completely in a pit in the sand. Only its pincer-like jaws stick out.

It flicks sand at passing ants to make them lose their footing and slide down the sloping sides of the pit.

The ant-lion strikes with a snap of its jaws. It devours the ant, then rebuilds its trap to wait for more prey.

Beetle bang

A bombardier beetle can aim a boiling-hot spray of toxic liquid to fend off an attacker. The spray shoots out with a loud bang. The chemicals in the spray are mixed together just before the beetle fires it. They react with each other to make the explosive noise and generate heat.

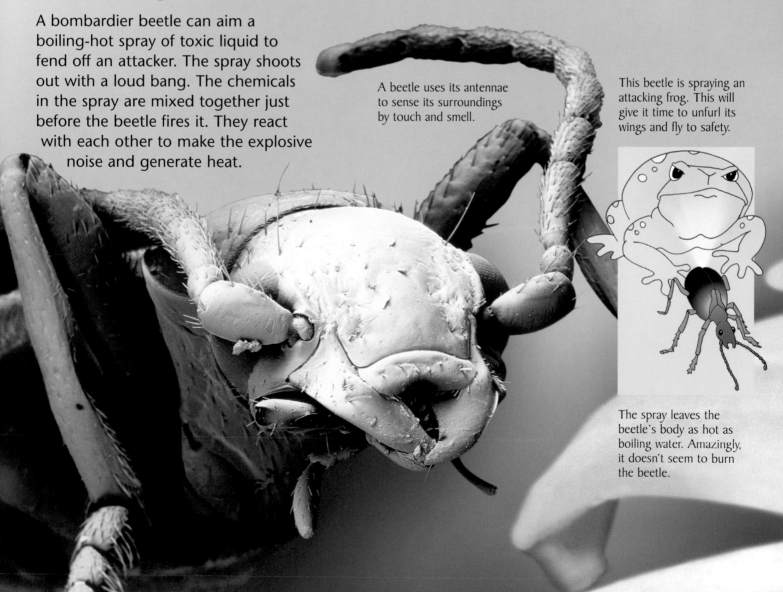

A beetle uses its antennae to sense its surroundings by touch and smell.

This beetle is spraying an attacking frog. This will give it time to unfurl its wings and fly to safety.

The spray leaves the beetle's body as hot as boiling water. Amazingly, it doesn't seem to burn the beetle.

Smelly spray

Darkling beetles use a spray of terrible-smelling liquid to defend themselves. If they are threatened, they crouch down, raise their back ends into the air and prepare to release their spray. Many animals avoid them because of their smell, but they are preyed on by owls, toads and skunks.

A darkling beetle tips its back end up and sprays an attacker with a foul-smelling liquid.

The beetle is quite slow. A predator such as a toad may be able to swallow it before it has time to spray.

A grasshopper mouse has a clever way of disarming the beetle. It pushes its dangerous back end into the ground and nibbles the front end.

INTERNET LINK
For a link to a website where you can find out more about the amazing bombardier beetle, go to www.usborne-quicklinks.com

An assassin bug holds its prey with its front legs and pierces it with its sharp beak.

This assassin bug is eating a crab spider. Sometimes assassin bugs even eat each other.

Assassin bugs have bright markings which warn other insects to beware of their poison.

Insect hitman

Assassin bugs get their name because of the way they ambush other small creatures. An assassin bug strikes quickly, grabbing its prey with its two front legs and using its sharp beak to inject saliva. The saliva immobilizes the victim and begins to dissolve its tissues. The bug can then suck up its victim's remains through its beak.

TRICKY PLANTS

Some plants use tricks and disguises to attract helpful small creatures, while others try to hide away for fear of being eaten. A few plants fight back against grazing animals with painful, acidic stings.

Living stones

Living stones come out of hiding when they flower – the bright flowers attract insects.

In the desert, juicy plants can be a source of moisture for thirsty animals. But living stone plants look just like small pebbles, blending in with their dry, rocky surroundings. Only a small part of the plant sticks up above the surface of the ground.

The only two parts of the living stone that poke above ground are the fleshy leaves.

The egg trick

Butterflies try to lay their eggs where their caterpillars will have plenty of food when they hatch. A good place is on the leaf of a tasty plant. To avoid becoming caterpillar food, some plants fight back.

Heliconius butterflies lay their eggs on passionflower vines, on the underside of the leaves.

When the eggs hatch, the caterpillars devour the plant, killing it in the process.

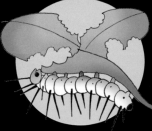

Butterflies tend not to lay eggs on leaves where there are eggs already. So one type of vine grows false eggs on its leaves, tricking butterflies into leaving it alone.

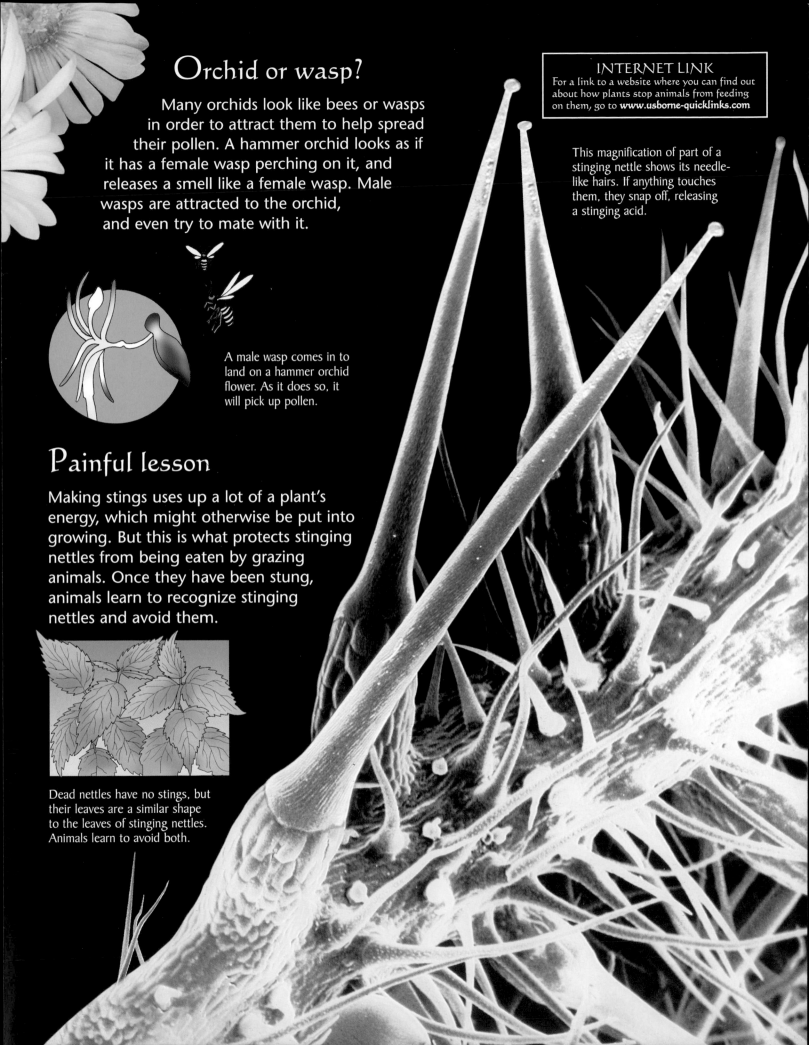

Orchid or wasp?

Many orchids look like bees or wasps in order to attract them to help spread their pollen. A hammer orchid looks as if it has a female wasp perching on it, and releases a smell like a female wasp. Male wasps are attracted to the orchid, and even try to mate with it.

A male wasp comes in to land on a hammer orchid flower. As it does so, it will pick up pollen.

Painful lesson

Making stings uses up a lot of a plant's energy, which might otherwise be put into growing. But this is what protects stinging nettles from being eaten by grazing animals. Once they have been stung, animals learn to recognize stinging nettles and avoid them.

Dead nettles have no stings, but their leaves are a similar shape to the leaves of stinging nettles. Animals learn to avoid both.

INTERNET LINK
For a link to a website where you can find out about how plants stop animals from feeding on them, go to www.usborne-quicklinks.com

This magnification of part of a stinging nettle shows its needle-like hairs. If anything touches them, they snap off, releasing a stinging acid.

SURVIVAL TRICKS

Many underwater creatures use camouflage to hide themselves from predators or prey. Others have early warning systems that give them time to escape or to unleash weapons on their attackers.

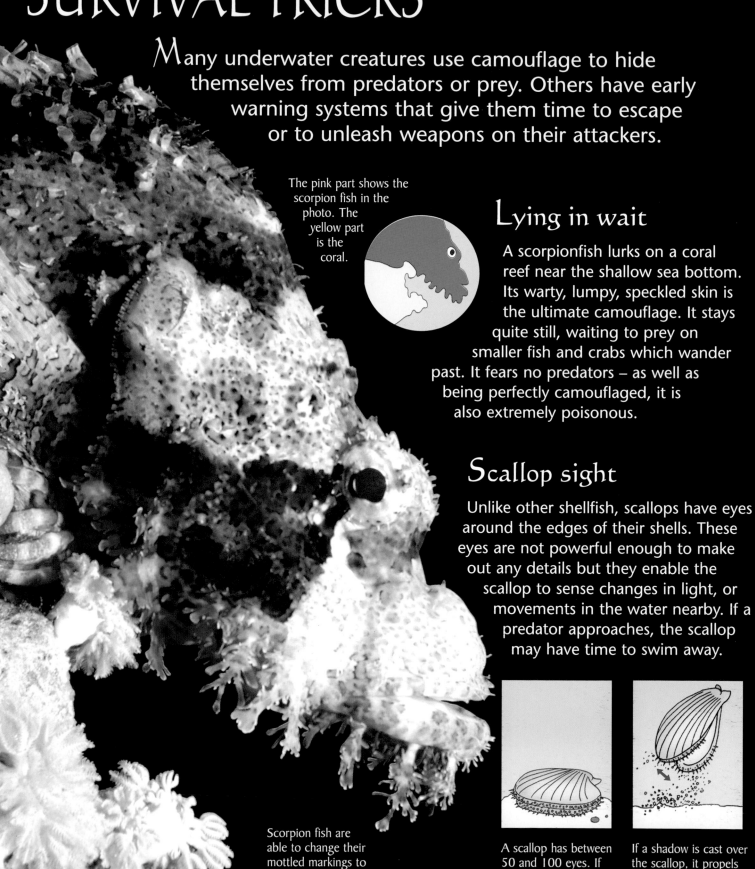

The pink part shows the scorpion fish in the photo. The yellow part is the coral.

Lying in wait

A scorpionfish lurks on a coral reef near the shallow sea bottom. Its warty, lumpy, speckled skin is the ultimate camouflage. It stays quite still, waiting to prey on smaller fish and crabs which wander past. It fears no predators – as well as being perfectly camouflaged, it is also extremely poisonous.

Scallop sight

Unlike other shellfish, scallops have eyes around the edges of their shells. These eyes are not powerful enough to make out any details but they enable the scallop to sense changes in light, or movements in the water nearby. If a predator approaches, the scallop may have time to swim away.

Scorpion fish are able to change their mottled markings to blend with their surroundings.

A scallop has between 50 and 100 eyes. If they sense movement, the scallop closes its shell.

If a shadow is cast over the scallop, it propels itself away through the water by flapping the two halves of its shell.

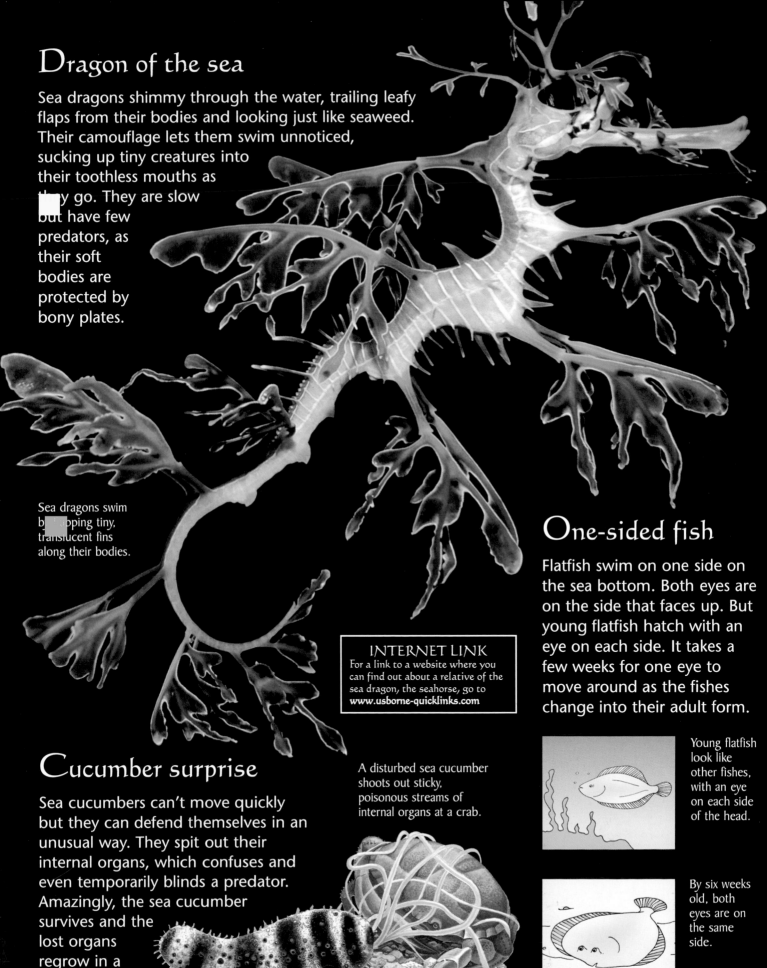

Dragon of the sea

Sea dragons shimmy through the water, trailing leafy flaps from their bodies and looking just like seaweed. Their camouflage lets them swim unnoticed, sucking up tiny creatures into their toothless mouths as they go. They are slow but have few predators, as their soft bodies are protected by bony plates.

Sea dragons swim by flapping tiny, translucent fins along their bodies.

One-sided fish

Flatfish swim on one side on the sea bottom. Both eyes are on the side that faces up. But young flatfish hatch with an eye on each side. It takes a few weeks for one eye to move around as the fishes change into their adult form.

INTERNET LINK
For a link to a website where you can find out about a relative of the sea dragon, the seahorse, go to
www.usborne-quicklinks.com

Young flatfish look like other fishes, with an eye on each side of the head.

By six weeks old, both eyes are on the same side.

Cucumber surprise

Sea cucumbers can't move quickly but they can defend themselves in an unusual way. They spit out their internal organs, which confuses and even temporarily blinds a predator. Amazingly, the sea cucumber survives and the lost organs regrow in a few weeks.

A disturbed sea cucumber shoots out sticky, poisonous streams of internal organs at a crab.

FIGHTING BACK

Reptiles have tough skins for protection, and unusual fighting weapons. Horned lizards can even squirt their own blood to put an enemy off. Reptiles and amphibians are also masters of camouflage.

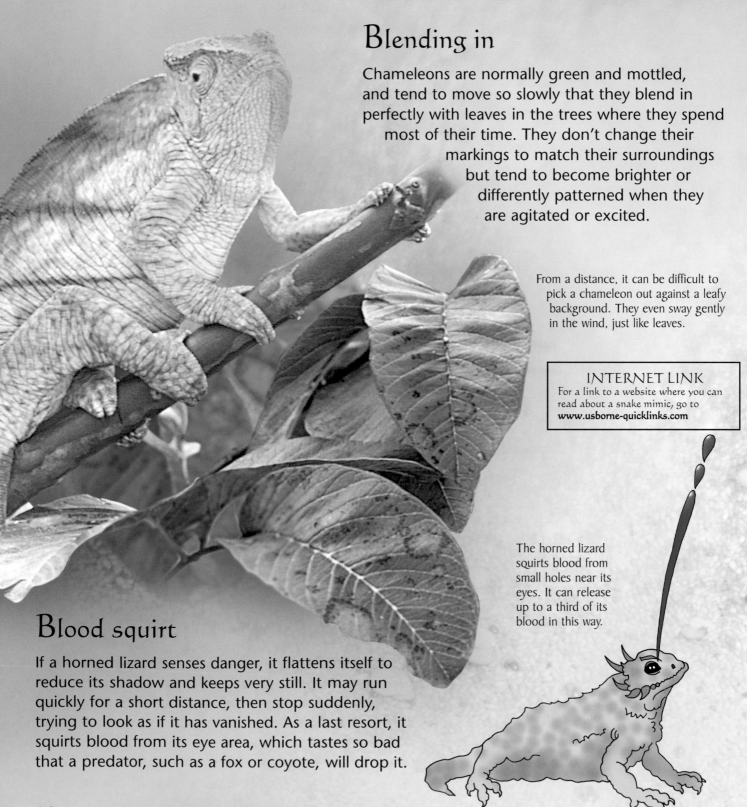

Blending in

Chameleons are normally green and mottled, and tend to move so slowly that they blend in perfectly with leaves in the trees where they spend most of their time. They don't change their markings to match their surroundings but tend to become brighter or differently patterned when they are agitated or excited.

From a distance, it can be difficult to pick a chameleon out against a leafy background. They even sway gently in the wind, just like leaves.

INTERNET LINK
For a link to a website where you can read about a snake mimic, go to
www.usborne-quicklinks.com

The horned lizard squirts blood from small holes near its eyes. It can release up to a third of its blood in this way.

Blood squirt

If a horned lizard senses danger, it flattens itself to reduce its shadow and keeps very still. It may run quickly for a short distance, then stop suddenly, trying to look as if it has vanished. As a last resort, it squirts blood from its eye area, which tastes so bad that a predator, such as a fox or coyote, will drop it.

46

Defensive tactics

Australian thorny devils may not look very tasty, with their all-over spiny covering, but they are still in danger from large birds. Apart from its prickles, a thorny devil has a few other tricks.

When scared or cold (and so unable to run fast), the thorny devil's markings become duller and help to camouflage it.

The thorny devil can inflate itself by taking gulps of air. This may deter a predator from trying to swallow it.

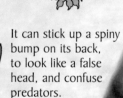

It can stick up a spiny bump on its back, to look like a false head, and confuse predators.

Hard to swallow

Armadillo lizards can't run very fast so they have to use other methods to outwit predators such as snakes or birds. They can, with a little effort, make themselves completely unswallowable.

A lizard may try to fight off attackers by rolling its tail up to form a club, which it can hit with.

It may curl up into a ball, with its spiny, bony back facing out. Its soft tummy is protected on the inside.

The lizard may squeeze into a rocky crevice to escape. It raises its spines so that it can't be pulled out from its hiding place.

Double camouflage

A bullfrog's green skin helps camouflage it in its swampy home, especially when it is submerged in duckweed with only its eyes showing above the water. From here, the frog is in the perfect position to stalk insect prey such as fireflies, bees and crickets. At the same time, it is hidden from its own predators such as herons, owls and hawks.

This bullfrog is well-hidden from birds, but there is also danger from muskrats, fishes and even larger bullfrogs under the water.

STAYING SAFE

Some birds put a lot of effort into building nests in places that are hard to reach. Others just make a small scrape in the ground to lay their eggs. Both adults and babies use camouflage and other tactics to protect themselves from attack.

Hidden in the sand

Black skimmers live near water and make very shallow nests on sandy beaches for their eggs. Their chicks are vulnerable out in the open, so they rely on excellent camouflage to protect themselves.

INTERNET LINK
For a link to a website where you can read an article about birds defending themselves, go to www.usborne-quicklinks.com

The eggs and chicks of black skimmers have mottled markings to help them blend in with beach sand and debris.

Snipe's stripes

A jack snipe uses the stripes on its body to help it to hide in the marshland where it lives. When it lands, it turns itself so that its stripes run in the same direction as the marsh grasses around it. This camouflage can be so successful that bird watchers sometimes tread on jack snipes by mistake.

If disturbed, the snipe flies off a little way, then drops down into the grass.

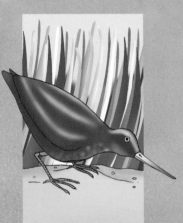

It crouches in the grass, where it will stay until the danger has passed.

It lines the stripes on its body up with the grasses around it for camouflage.

Feisty chicks

Fulmars leave their chicks alone while they go fishing at sea. The chicks might need to fight off attacks by skuas, eagles and gulls. They do this by spitting a smelly substance which destroys the waterproofing of the attacking bird's feathers. Even parent birds approach carefully until their chicks can recognize them.

If a fulmar chick is threatened, it spits a smelly orange substance at its attacker, over a distance of up to 1.5m (5ft).

Through the spring, more brown feathers appear as white ones are lost.

By the time summer arrives, all the ptarmigan's feathers are brown.

In spring, the snow melts and the ptarmigan starts to lose its white feathers.

Winter wear

Ptarmigans live on the ground in tundra regions, which are covered in snow for half the year. They are in danger from eagles, owls and other birds of prey from the air, and foxes and coyotes on the ground. To make sure that they always blend into the landscape, ptarmigans change their plumage with the seasons.

A ptarmigan in winter plumage blends into the snow.

CONFUSE OR DEFEND

All mammals have fur or hair on their bodies. It can help them defend themselves in a number of ways, usually by providing camouflage. Mammals have other ways, too, of outwitting attackers or making sure that they leave them alone.

Secret of the stripes

It may seem to us that zebras stand out against the green and yellow of their grassland home. But their main predators, lions, can only see in black and white. The zebra's stripy coat blends in with the way the grasses grow, providing excellent camouflage.

Zebras may use their striped coats to recognize each other. No two have the same pattern.

Herd on the run

Zebras' stripes can also confuse predators. Once a herd of zebras starts moving, their striped coats seem to merge together. This makes it very difficult for a predator such as a lion to pick out a single zebra to chase.

INTERNET LINK
For a link to a website where you can play a game to learn more about camouflage, go to **www.usborne-quicklinks.com**

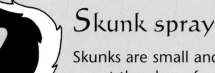

Skunk spray

Skunks are small and can't move very fast, yet they have few enemies. If it feels threatened, the skunk moves into a warning position. This is an attacker's last chance to escape before the skunk lets off a spray of extremely smelly, acidic liquid. Most animals have learned to stay away from the skunk because of this.

A skunk can spray up to 4.5m (15ft). The spray may temporarily blind an attacker.

If a skunk feels threatened, it raises its tail as a warning.

Bony ball

Three-banded armadillos are covered in bony plates. By rolling into a ball, an armadillo becomes completely protected on the outside, with its soft belly tucked away inside. A rolled-up armadillo is safe from most predators. It's still vulnerable to jaguars, though, which might be able to crack open the hard shell.

An armadillo's soft belly is vulnerable until it rolls up.

The armadillo leaves a crack open wide enough to pinch an intruding paw.

Hollow hairs

A polar bear looks white, but its hairs are actually clear tubes. These reflect light to make the bear look white or cream, so it blends in with its icy surroundings. The hollow hairs trap and magnify the Sun's rays, which helps to keep the bear warm. Surprisingly, the bear's skin is black, which also absorbs heat.

Heat from sunlight travels down the hollow hairs to the bear's black skin.

TRICKS AND MIMICS

Insects are often much smaller than their enemies, so they use camouflage, mimicry and tricks to avoid danger. Some have disguises that are realistic enough to frighten their attackers away.

Giant eyes

Caterpillars make juicy meals. If a puss moth caterpillar is threatened, it pulls in its head and inflates part of its body. The skin on this part has eyespot markings which look huge and scary when the segments bulge.

Beneath its waving tails, a puss moth caterpillar hides short, poisonous spines.

Moving thorns

Treehoppers live on plants and suck their juices.

If disturbed, a treehopper jumps away with a snapping noise.

Treehoppers are insects with large, pointed outer cases. They look like thorns as they walk on the stems of plants. They have few enemies. Spiders can't bite through their hard covering and they are too spiny for birds to swallow.

To alarm predators, the caterpillar weaves its body from side to side like a snake.

Wrong end

If a butterfly is pecked by a bird, it is less damaging to be pecked on the edge of a wing than on its head. This is why a hairstreak butterfly has false antennae on the ends of its wings, which it uses to confuse predators.

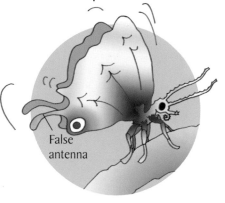

False antenna

A hairstreak butterfly lands and flaps its wings. This makes its false antennae move and look real.

A bird pecks the butterfly. It is confused by the false antennae and attacks the wrong end.

The butterfly flies away from danger but not in the direction that its attacker, confused by the false antennae, expects.

Owl eyes

Owl butterflies come out to find fruit at dusk. To avoid being eaten by small birds, they have owl-like markings. Small birds usually stay well away from anything that looks like an owl, in case they get eaten themselves. If a small bird does attack an owl butterfly, it usually goes for the eye markings on the wings and not the butterfly's body.

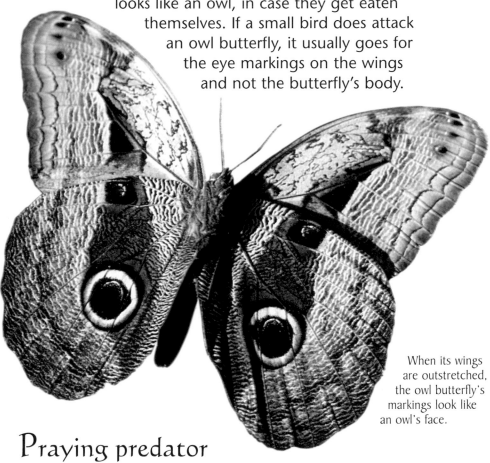

When its wings are outstretched, the owl butterfly's markings look like an owl's face.

Praying predator

A praying mantis uses its camouflage to hunt by stealth. It stands very still on a twig or branch, looking like a small twig itself, and waits for passing insect prey. It holds its lethal front legs together, and looks as if it is praying. This is how the insect got its name.

A praying mantis has sharp spikes on its front legs which it uses to grab its prey.

INTERNET LINK
For a link to a website with lots of general, fun facts about bugs, go to
www.usborne-quicklinks.com

HELP OR HINDER

Some plants and animals live alongside each other and help each other out. But the relationship may be one-sided. A plant or animal that takes what it needs without giving anything in return is called a parasite.

Musical tree

Whistling thorn acacias provide homes for ants. At the bases of their thorns, there are hollow balls called ant galls. Ants live inside these.

If a tree is disturbed by a grazing animal, ants rush out of the ant galls and bite the animal, which sends it away.

Some ant galls are abandoned, leaving only hollow balls with holes. When the wind blows through them, it makes a whistling sound.

Acacias and ants

Bull's horn acacia trees provide the ants living inside their thorns with food and nectar. The food is in bundles on the ends of the leaves. Nectar comes in pots called nectaries at the bases of the leaves. In return, the ants protect the acacia. If an animal tries to eat the tree's leaves, ants swarm out and bite it.

INTERNET LINK
For a link to a website where you can find out more about relationships between plants and creatures, go to
www.usborne-quicklinks.com

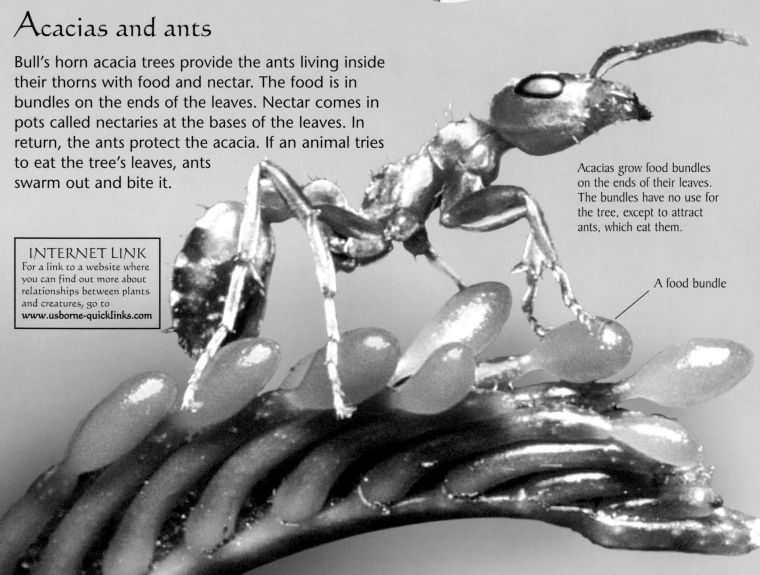

Acacias grow food bundles on the ends of their leaves. The bundles have no use for the tree, except to attract ants, which eat them.

A food bundle

Mobile home

Tiny plants called algae grow inside a sloth's hollow hairs, which makes its fur look green. This helps the sloth blend in with the forest greenery and so it is less likely to be spotted by predators. The algae benefit from the relationship by getting a place to live.

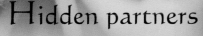

Hidden partners

Truffles are fungi that grow on tree roots underground. They take food from the tree but they also help it by releasing nutrients into the soil for it to use. Animals help truffles reproduce by carrying their spores to new places.

A sloth's green-tinged fur helps it to hide. The sloth keeps still and may look like part of the tree it is hanging from.

A truffle grows on the root of an oak tree. To grow, it takes nutrients from the tree and also from the soil.

A pig is attracted to the strong smell produced by the truffle. It digs it up and eats it.

Spores from the truffle pass out in the pig's droppings, in a new place. New truffles may grow.

Space invasion

Not all relationships between living things are good for both. Strangler figs start off as small hitchhikers on larger trees. They use the tree for support, although they get nutrients from the ground through their own roots. But there is not enough light or water for two, and eventually the fig kills the other tree.

A strangler fig starts to grow from a seed dropped on a tree branch. The seed sprouts leaves and sends a shoot down to the ground.

The shoot reaches the ground and takes root. The fig gets water and nutrients from the soil, and wraps itself around the host tree.

The fig competes with its host for light, water and nutrients. It grows stronger and squeezes the tree to death. Only the fig is left.

55

OCEAN PARTNERS

Many sea creatures have relationships with others. In some partnerships, both sides benefit. In others, one partner slowly saps the other's strength and may even end up killing it.

Contract cleaning

Cleaner wrasse set up "cleaning stations" where other fish come to have pests and dead skin nibbled away. The wrasse clean between scales and inside the gills and mouths of bigger fish, and get a meal in the process. The bigger fish get a good clean, and in return for this, don't eat the wrasse.

Fish line up to visit a group of cleaner wrasse.

A cleaner wrasse may clean 2,500 clients in a day.

Poisonous protection

A clownfish can shelter among the poisonous tentacles of a sea anemone without getting stung. The fish coats itself in the anemone's own slime, tricking the anemone. The clownfish helps the anemone, too, by luring its own predators closer, for the anemone to trap and eat.

A clownfish must stay near the anemone and return to it carefully. If it loses its coating of slime, it can be stung like any other fish.

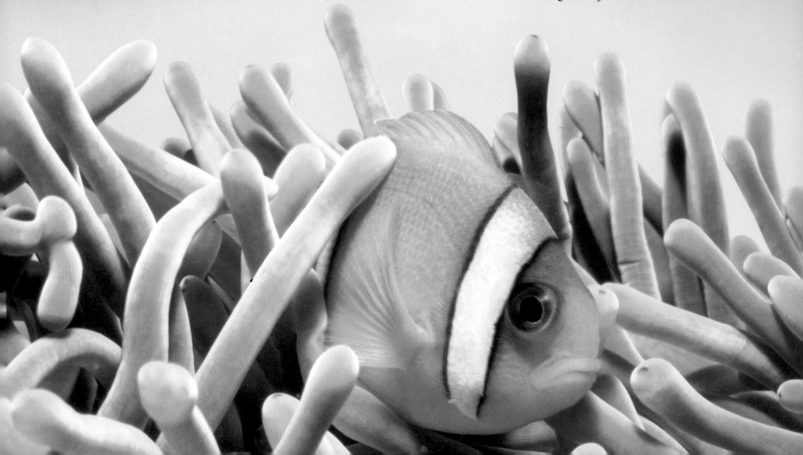

Team cleaning

Like cleaner wrasse, some shrimps set up cleaning stations. They wave their antennae to attract clients. Often the shrimps work in pairs. They pay special attention to the teeth of their clients. They have even been known to clean the teeth of human divers.

A cleaner shrimp picks scraps of food away from the razor-sharp teeth of a moray eel.

Intestine intruder

A sea cucumber can't defend itself against a parasitic pearlfish. Given the chance, the pearlfish wriggles tail-first inside the sea cucumber and snacks on its intestines. The cucumber doesn't benefit from the relationship but its internal organs do grow back after being eaten.

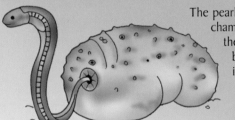

The pearlfish enters a chamber at the back of the sea cucumber's body, and lives inside.

The pearlfish may leave the sea cucumber to find other food, but it later returns to its host.

Flashing fish

A flashlight fish has pouches under its eyes, where light-producing bacteria live. The bacteria feed on the fish's blood. In return, they produce a bright light that can help the fish confuse an enemy. The fish turns the lights on and off by moving a flap of skin over each pouch.

If threatened by a hungry squid, the flashlight fish swims in one direction with its lights shining.

It then covers the light and rapidly changes direction, which confuses the squid.

INTERNET LINK
For a link to a website where you can find out more about coral reef cleaning stations, go to
www.usborne-quicklinks.com

57

SHARING SPACES

Reptiles are not naturally sociable creatures. But some form partnerships with other animals. They may share a nest, or hitch a ride. Crocodiles even get their teeth cleaned by small birds.

Plucky plover

Without its teeth, a crocodile would be unable to catch or eat food, and so it would die. But food scraps stuck between its teeth cause tooth decay, and parasitic leeches feed on its gums. Birds called plovers sometimes pick at the food scraps and parasites around a crocodile's teeth. They get an easy meal and the crocodile gets its teeth cleaned.

A plover picks at food scraps and pests between a crocodile's teeth.

Some plovers also pick irritating parasites off the crocodile's back.

The turtle's long claws help it hang onto the alligator's back.

Well-timed trip

Hungry alligators eat mainly fish but they may snap up any creatures that pass their way. A well-fed alligator is no threat to a turtle, though, and may even provide it with a free ride.

Borrowed burrow

Gopher tortoises dig large burrows to live in. They share their burrows with lots of different creatures – some friends, some foes. Up to 360 different species have been found in a burrow, including snakes, owls, armadillos, opossums, frogs and mice. Some of these help the tortoise keep its burrow clean.

A gopher tortoise digs a burrow that is as wide as the tortoise is long, so that it can turn around inside.

A gopher tortoise can block a pine snake intruder with its shell.

Gopher frogs eat insects that come into the burrow.

A visiting armadillo may eat the tortoise's eggs.

Gopher mice eat seeds that fall into the burrow.

Dangerous guest

Tuataras are lizard-like reptiles. They often share the burrows of sea birds called petrels. Both are night animals. The tuatara eats insects that live in the burrow but it may also eat the petrel's eggs, chicks, or even the petrel itself.

INTERNET LINK
For a link to a website about a reptile's relationship with an owl, go to www.usborne-quicklinks.com

Both the tuatara and the petrel leave their shared burrow at night, to find food.

As the petrel flies in and out of the burrow, it stirs up insects, which the tuatara eats.

FINDING FOOD

Some birds hitch rides on other animals, or follow them, to find food. Sometimes the birds help the other creatures out in return, but not always.

Bird on bird

The picture shows a carmine bee-eater perching on the back of a kori bustard. As the heavy bustard tramples through grass, insects fly up to get out of its way. These are snapped up by the bee-eater. In return, the bee-eater warns the bustard of danger, as it will fly away if it spots predators.

In return for easy meals, the little bee-eater provides the bustard with an early-warning system. It will fly away if it spots a predator such as a lion, leopard or eagle.

Useful ants

Army ants work together in huge groups, and catch insects, frogs and even small mammals. Antbirds follow army ants, using them like a pack of hunting dogs to flush out prey. The most senior antbird follows the biggest army of ants, and so has the best chance of finding the most prey.

A column of army ants marches through a rainforest. An antbird runs and hops alongside them.

The army disturbs other insects and small animals. They must move, or risk being eaten by the ants.

The antbird snaps up some of the escaping insects with its slender beak.

60

Honey helpers

Honey guide birds eat honey, bee larvae and wax. They can't get into bees' nests on their own, though, so they seek the help of another creature – the honey badger.

Honey badgers eat almost anything they can find but they love honey most of all. They will happily follow a honey guide bird, knowing that it will lead them to a supply of honey. The badger breaks into the nest and the bird can eat, too. In this way, the two creatures help each other.

This honey guide bird has found a bees' nest in a tree. It will now look for a honey badger to help it open up the nest.

The honey badger follows the honey guide to the bees' nest. The badger rips open the nest with its sharp claws.

The badger feeds first, on honey. It leaves behind wax, bee larvae and some of the honey, for the honey guide.

Food on the move

Red-billed oxpeckers live near large animals on the African grasslands. They feed on the ticks, fleas and flies that live on cattle, elephants, giraffe, rhinos and antelopes. They also nibble at the animals' dead skin, mucus, saliva, sweat and especially their blood. Oxpeckers may help their host animals by getting rid of their parasites, but they will also nibble at an animal's wound, so it takes longer to heal.

INTERNET LINK
For a link to a website where you can read about how birds make their intelligence work for them, go to
www.usborne-quicklinks.com

A red-billed oxpecker eats parasites from places such as the inside of the ear, which this greater kudu can't reach with its own teeth.

MAMMALS' FRIENDS

Some mammals have relationships with plants or other animals that help them to survive. Their partners usually get something in return, like a share in the food or a place to live.

Useful bats

Many rainforest bats eat fruit. They pass the seeds of the fruit out in their droppings. For some fruit trees, this is the main way of spreading their seeds to new places.

Plants with pale flowers that come out at night tend to attract bats. The bats carry pollen on their fur from one plant to another, helping the plants to make seeds and reproduce.

This scary-looking bat only eats fruit. It uses its teeth to spear and grip the fruit.

Flowers that bloom at night are usually pale so they show up in the dark.

As a bat licks nectar from a night-blooming flower, pollen coats its furry body.

When it moves on to the next plant to feed, the pollen will rub off.

Useful ants

A pangolin's tough scales protect it, but also hide lice and other pests that the pangolin can't reach. Although a pangolin is an anteater, it may take a break from eating ants and instead let them clean it. The ants crawl in between its scales, eating the pests.

When the pangolin lifts its scales, ants can crawl underneath and eat lice and other pests.

Fishing together

Fishermen and river dolphins in the Irrawaddy River in Myanmar work together to increase their catch of fish. Their relationship has developed over hundreds of years. Both sides benefit from the partnership.

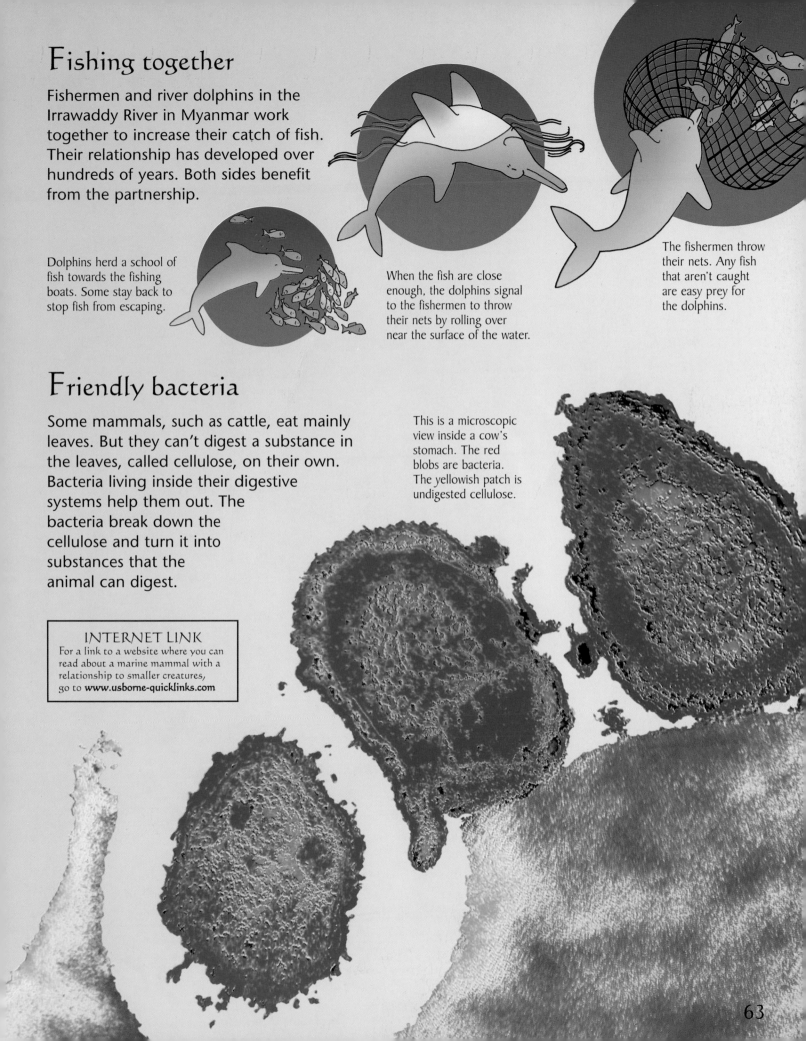

Dolphins herd a school of fish towards the fishing boats. Some stay back to stop fish from escaping.

When the fish are close enough, the dolphins signal to the fishermen to throw their nets by rolling over near the surface of the water.

The fishermen throw their nets. Any fish that aren't caught are easy prey for the dolphins.

Friendly bacteria

Some mammals, such as cattle, eat mainly leaves. But they can't digest a substance in the leaves, called cellulose, on their own. Bacteria living inside their digestive systems help them out. The bacteria break down the cellulose and turn it into substances that the animal can digest.

This is a microscopic view inside a cow's stomach. The red blobs are bacteria. The yellowish patch is undigested cellulose.

INTERNET LINK
For a link to a website where you can read about a marine mammal with a relationship to smaller creatures, go to www.usborne-quicklinks.com

MEAL DEALS

INTERNET LINK
For a link to a website where you can find out more about nectar-robbing bees, go to www.usborne-quicklinks.com

Many kinds of insects go into partnerships with plants. In return for a supply of sweet nectar, the insects carry pollen from one plant to another. This enables the plants to make seeds and reproduce.

This bee has been drinking nectar from a flower. Fine pollen grains have rubbed off the flower onto the hairs on its body and legs.

Something for nothing

Unlike most bees, nectar-robbing bees are distinctly unhelpful to plants. They use their biting mouthparts to break into flowers and steal their nectar, without picking up and passing on the plant's pollen.

Once the nectar is gone, other creatures won't visit the plant. It doesn't receive pollen from another plant, so it can't make seeds.

A hummingbird sips nectar from a gilia plant's long, trumpet-shaped flowers. At the same time, it picks up and passes on pollen.

A nectar-robbing bee bites into a gilia flower. It drinks the nectar but doesn't pick up pollen. Hummingbirds won't visit, and pollinate, a robbed flower.

Live and let live

Yucca plants and yucca moths have to live together – in fact, they can't live without each other. This is because only yucca moths can pollinate yucca plants. In return, the moths get somewhere to lay their eggs – on the yuccas' flowers. When the eggs hatch, the caterpillars feed on the yucca plant's seeds. They can't survive on any other plant.

A female yucca moth visits different yucca plants' flowers, collecting pollen from each one. She rolls it together to form a ball, which she keeps under her chin.

The yucca moth stuffs pollen from the ball she has made into the female parts of other yuccas' flowers. They can then make seeds and reproduce.

64

Hidden flowers

A fig is not a real fruit, but is actually a fleshy bundle of flowers. These flowers can only be pollinated by a certain kind of female wasp, called a fig wasp. She wriggles inside the fig through a tiny hole, ripping her wings off in the process. She pollinates the flowers with pollen collected from a different fig, lays her eggs and then dies.

Egg-laying tube

This parasitic wasp lays its eggs in figs but doesn't burrow into or pollinate them. Instead, it pierces the fig with its long egg-laying tube.

A female fig wasp squeezes into a fig to lay her eggs. Young wasps will hatch and mate with each other.

The females then leave to find new figs to pollinate. The males are wingless and can never escape.

Fig wasp

Female fig wasp leaving

Bug farmers

Aphids suck plant juices and produce a kind of sweet, milky white liquid, made up of excess sugar. This is called honeydew and ants love it. Ants "farm" groups of aphids almost like people farm cows. They protect the aphids from other creatures in order to keep for themselves all the honeydew that the aphids produce.

An ant guards its flock of aphids. It feeds on the honeydew that they produce.

Aphids feed using piercing and sucking mouthparts. They multiply very quickly.

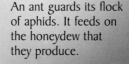

PLANT COMMUNITIES

The place where a plant grows naturally is called its habitat. Some plants and animals share the same habitat. They live together in communities.

Tank tenants

Tank bromeliads are plants that live perched high up on the branches of rainforest trees. They can't collect water from the ground so their waxy leaves form a cup, which collects a pool of rainwater. The tank also collects leaf litter from nearby trees, and gives a home to a collection of small animals.

A tank bromeliad shares its tank with visitors such as small frogs, insects and even a type of crab that only lives in bromeliads.

Tree frogs feast on insects that drop into the bromeliad's tank.

Two-in-one plants

A lichen is not just one plant but two – an alga and a fungus. They can't survive without each other. The fungus part provides a sturdy base for the alga to grow on, and soaks up water and food. In return, the alga uses sunlight to make food for itself and the fungus.

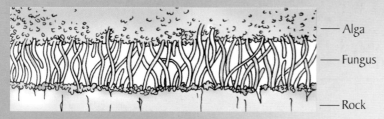

— Alga

— Fungus

— Rock

Lichens are slow-growing but are able to live in places where other plants can't, such as tree bark or the surface of rocks.

Lichens grow in many different shapes. Some, like this one, are flat and crust-like. Others are more leafy.

INTERNET LINK
For a link to a website where you can find out more about mangroves, go to www.usborne-quicklinks.com

Interlinked life

A rainforest is a huge ecosystem in which many thousands of plant and animal species live.

Communities of animals and plants living together are called an ecosystem. A rainforest is an ecosystem. A hedgerow is a much smaller example. Within ecosystems, plants and animals may depend on each other. The loss of a plant community from an ecosystem has an impact on the animals that live in it, endangering their survival.

Cutting down areas of rainforest kills the trees and plants that grew there. It would take centuries for many of these trees to grow back.

Animals that lived in the deforested area must find new homes or else they will die.

Many-homed mangroves

Mangroves are trees that grow along coastlines and riverbanks. They have large bundles of roots to anchor themselves in the waterlogged, muddy ground. They provide a home for many creatures. Herons and sea birds roost in their branches. Mangrove crabs creep around on their trunks. Oysters, barnacles and sponges cling to partly-submerged roots. Fish lurk among the roots underwater.

Fish use the mangrove roots as a place to hide from predators that are too big to squeeze through the gaps.

These mangroves are growing in a lake.

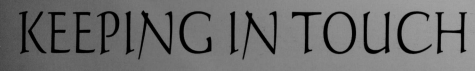

KEEPING IN TOUCH

Many fish gather in huge groups, called shoals, as they move through the ocean. For some, this provides safety in numbers. Others get together to hunt. Members of a group need to be able to communicate with one another. They use body language, markings and sound to keep in touch.

Losing touch

A shoal of small fish moving together may look like a single large animal, and an individual fish is less likely to be eaten if it is surrounded by others. Hunting barracudas weave in and out of shoals of smaller fish to break up their group and confuse them. A lone fish is easy prey for a barracuda, with its fiercely snapping teeth.

Barracudas can't open their mouths wide so they use sharp teeth to slash their prey.

One fish has become separated from the rest of the shoal. The barracuda singles this out.

Each fish has a sense organ called a lateral line, which lets it sense where other fish are. The lateral line runs along its body.

INTERNET LINK
For a link to a website where you can listen to recordings of the songs of humpback whales, go to **www.usborne-quicklinks.com**

68

Mood markings

Cuttlefish change their markings depending on their mood, which allows them to communicate with other cuttlefish. Most of the time, they blend into their surroundings. But to attract a mate, a male puts on a display of flickering patterns.

A cuttlefish's skin has cells filled with pigments, which expand and contract very quickly to make different patterns.

Long song

Humpback whales make moans, squeals and clicks to communicate with each other. But during the breeding season, males also sing complex songs to entice females and ward off rivals. A humpback whale's song can be heard by other whales up to 160km (100 miles) away. Humpback whales also show their emotions using dramatic body language.

Humpbacks leap out of the water, then fall back with a huge splash. This is called breaching.

They splash their long flippers against the surface of the water.

Versatile voices

Dolphins use sounds to communicate with each other, and to build up a picture of their surroundings. Each dolphin can make a unique whistle to identify itself to others. They can also make sounds to confuse fish and even knock them out.

Huge tail fins, called flukes, make a very dramatic splash on the surface of the water.

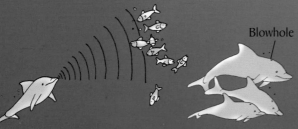

Blowhole

Dolphins use echoes to sense their surroundings, including the position of fish shoals nearby.

Dolphins make noises inside their blowholes to communicate with each other.

CALLS AND SIGNALS

Reptiles and amphibians have some remarkable ways of communicating. They might use these to attract a mate, for instance, or to warn off enemies.

Croc conversations

Crocodiles, alligators, gharials and caimans are the noisiest reptiles. They make many different sounds, including distress calls, courtship bellows and defensive hisses. Alligators can bellow loudly. You can see how they do this on the right.

To threaten an enemy, a crocodile may combine a defensive hiss with a snap of its fearsome jaws.

As the alligator starts to bellow, the rumbling sounds make ripples on the surface of the water.

It waves its tail from side to side. It also starts to make the air inside its closed mouth vibrate.

The alligator takes in air and raises its head and tail out of the water.

INTERNET LINK
For a link to a website about how crocodiles, alligators, caimans and gharials communicate, go to
www.usborne-quicklinks.com

Turn it up

Male frogs make loud calls. Large frogs make low-pitched croaks and small frogs make high-pitched squeaks. They call to attract a mate, to mark their territory or to show fear. One type of tree frog climbs inside hollow trees to amplify its call – like sitting inside a drum.

Some male frogs have throat pouches that help make their calls louder.

Touchy turtles

During the breeding season, a male painted turtle will try to charm a female into mating with him by gently caressing her cheeks with the long claws on his front legs. She will show if she is willing to mate with him by stroking his front legs in return.

A male swims up behind a female painted turtle and overtakes her.

He turns to face her. She keeps swimming, pushing him with her.

The male strokes the female's cheeks with his claws to see if she will mate.

Hooded warning

A cobra uses its hood to show anger or fear. The hood is made of skin stretched over ribs which can be raised to stand out around the snake's head. The cobra shows its hood to warn an animal that it may strike, with a deadly bite, if the animal doesn't escape quickly.

To scare an enemy into leaving it alone, a cobra makes its hood stand out, rears up and starts to sway and hiss.

If the enemy does not leave immediately after this warning, the snake will strike.

SHOWING OFF

Birds are great show-offs when it comes to attracting a mate. A male bird needs to prove to females that he is the best. He might get himself noticed by his bright feathers, or try to impress by performing a complicated dance to show how fit he is.

Interior design

Bowerbirds are the only creatures that use objects to impress the opposite sex – apart from humans. Male bowerbirds build dens, or bowers, out of twigs and grasses. They decorate them with leaves, flowers and feathers. They even use bottletops, plastic forks and other thrown-away things. When a female arrives at a bower, the male shows her his collection of objects. If she likes his display, they mate.

Satin bowerbirds paint the inside of their bower with the juice from blue berries.

They prefer to use blue objects to decorate their bowers.

This aracari's markings are made by pigments in its feathers.

Blue feathers shimmer in the light. This is called iridescence.

Fitness test

Many male birds use bright feathers to impress females. The fitter the bird, the brighter its plumage – and the fittest bird attracts the most mates.

Yellow, red, brown and black feathers contain pigments which a bird gets by eating certain fruits or seeds. Other feathers appear green or blue because of the way they reflect light.

Yellow feathers get their appearance from pigments in the bird's food.

Fashion shows

Male birds of paradise have vivid feathers, loud calls, and perform flamboyant dances, all in the hope of attracting a mate. Some birds even prepare a stage. They remove leaves from the area where they are going to dance, to increase their chances of being seen.

As a Raggiana bird of paradise displays its bright, velvety plumage, it also shrieks louder and louder.

Prince Rudolph birds of paradise hang upside-down to show off their feathers.

King of Saxony birds of paradise have two metallic-looking head feathers, 60cm (2ft) long, which wave as they bounce on branches.

Bowerbirds collect these feathers when birds shed them, to decorate their bowers.

INTERNET LINK
For a link to a website where you can find out how birds use song to communicate, go to www.usborne-quicklinks.com

73

FRIEND OR FOE

Many mammals live in groups. They defend each other against enemies, get rid of each others' parasites and form friendships and rivalries. They keep in touch using sounds and body language.

Each lemur in a group keeps its tail raised, to let the others know where it is at all times.

Touching teeth

Prairie dogs live in groups of thousands or even millions, called towns. Each town is divided into areas called wards, then into family groups called coteries. A coterie consists of a male, several females and their children. Prairie dogs touch teeth when they meet, to find out if they are from the same coterie.

The diagram below shows how a prairie dog town is divided into smaller groups.

```
                    Town
                      |
        ┌─────────────┼─────────────┐
       Ward          Ward          Ward
      ┌───┴───┐    ┌───┴───┐    ┌───┴───┐
  Coterie Coterie Coterie Coterie Coterie Coterie
```

Furry flag

Ring-tailed lemurs live in groups. They use their tails as markers to keep track of one another.

During the breeding season, males have scent battles. They rub their wrists against scent glands under their armpits, and coat their tails with the smelly substance. Then they wave their tails at each other in a threatening way, wafting the scent through the air.

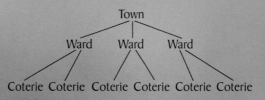

When prairie dogs meet, it looks as if they kiss, but they are actually touching teeth.

Lemurs coat their tails with scent, then wave their tails to fan the scents at each other.

Grins and grimaces

The most important male mandrill in a group has bright blue and red patches on his face and body, which become even brighter when the mandrill is excited. Most mandrills, though, communicate using facial expressions and body language. But these expressions may not mean what you expect...

A yawn doesn't indicate boredom but is a warning – the mandrill is frustrated or about to attack.

A toothy grimace may look threatening but it is really a sign of friendship.

Groom mates

Chimpanzees spend a lot of time grooming each other to remove dead skin, dirt and parasites from each others' coats. Shared grooming also helps the chimpanzees to make friends, comfort each other and sort out fights. A chimpanzee who has been away for a few days will be greeted by his friends on his return with a long grooming session.

Chimps' fingers are good at picking pests and dirt from the hair and skin.

INTERNET LINK
For a link to a website where you can read an article about chimpanzee communication, go to www.usborne-quicklinks.com

TEAM WORK

Some insects live in large, well-organized groups called colonies. Each colony is controlled by a queen who is looked after by workers. She is the only insect in the colony to lay eggs. Every other insect has its own special tasks, to make sure that the colony runs smoothly.

These worker bees are tending the six-sided wax cells of the comb.

Honeypots on legs

Some honey ant workers, called "honeypots", store huge amounts of nectar inside their bodies. They stay inside the nest and other workers feed them. They gradually become filled with nectar. This sugary store can be shared between all the ants in the colony when food is scarce.

Honeypot ants can't leave the underground chambers where they live – they are too fat.

Hive of activity

Worker honeybees only live for about a month in the summer. They work so hard in that time that they die of exhaustion.

Their duties in the beehive change as they grow older. The oldest worker bees guard the hive and look for food.

Newly-hatched workers clean the hive's wax cells.

After a week, the workers start to care for the queen.

After two weeks, they start building new honeycomb.

Finding food

Honeybee scouts fly away from their hive to find food. When they return, they tell the rest of the colony what they have found by performing a dance, which the others bees follow by touch. Inside a beehive it is dark, and bees are almost deaf, so this is the best way to communicate.

To encourage other bees in the hive to go out and forage for food, scout bees perform a round dance. They circle in one direction or the other.

Scout bees perform the "waggle dance" to show how far away a source of food is. This is in the rough shape of a figure eight.

The middle of the eight is angled to show the direction of the food. As the bee walks along this line, it waggles. The more vigorous the waggling, the closer the food source is.

Egg-machine queen

Queen termites are little more than egg-laying machines. Some can lay up to 30,000 eggs every day. A queen can be up to 12cm (5in) long – much bigger than the other termites in the colony.

A queen termite is so big that she can't move. She relies on workers to feed her, clean her and care for her eggs.

INTERNET LINK
For a link to a website where you can find out more about the honeybees' waggle dance, go to **www.usborne-quicklinks.com**

NEW PLANTS

Plants and fungi can reproduce in two ways. Asexual reproduction happens when part of a plant breaks away to form a miniature, identical plant. Sexual reproduction happens when two plant cells join together to make a seed, from which a new plant grows. This new plant is different from its parents.

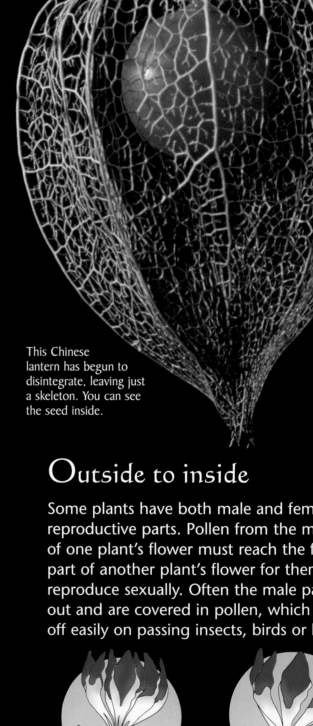

This Chinese lantern has begun to disintegrate, leaving just a skeleton. You can see the seed inside.

Flying lanterns

Chinese lantern plants have red, papery wrappers around their seeds that work like kites. They catch the wind and carry the seeds far away from the parent plants. When the seeds land, they start to grow into new plants. The seed-wrappers look like Chinese paper lanterns, which is how the plant got its name.

Pistil

Stamen

This flame lily has prominent stamens, which are the male parts, tipped with pollen. This rubs off if an insect touches it.

Outside to inside

Some plants have both male and female reproductive parts. Pollen from the male part of one plant's flower must reach the female part of another plant's flower for them to reproduce sexually. Often the male parts stick out and are covered in pollen, which brushes off easily on passing insects, birds or bats.

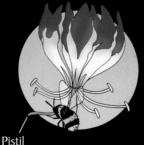

Pistil

Pollen brushes off the insect onto the sticky pistil – the female part of another lily.

Seed

The pollen travels down the pistil, deep inside the flower. This is where the seeds form.

Mini adult

Plants reproduce asexually in different ways. Most involve a small part of the parent plant sending out roots to form a new, separate plant. The new plant is identical to its parent.

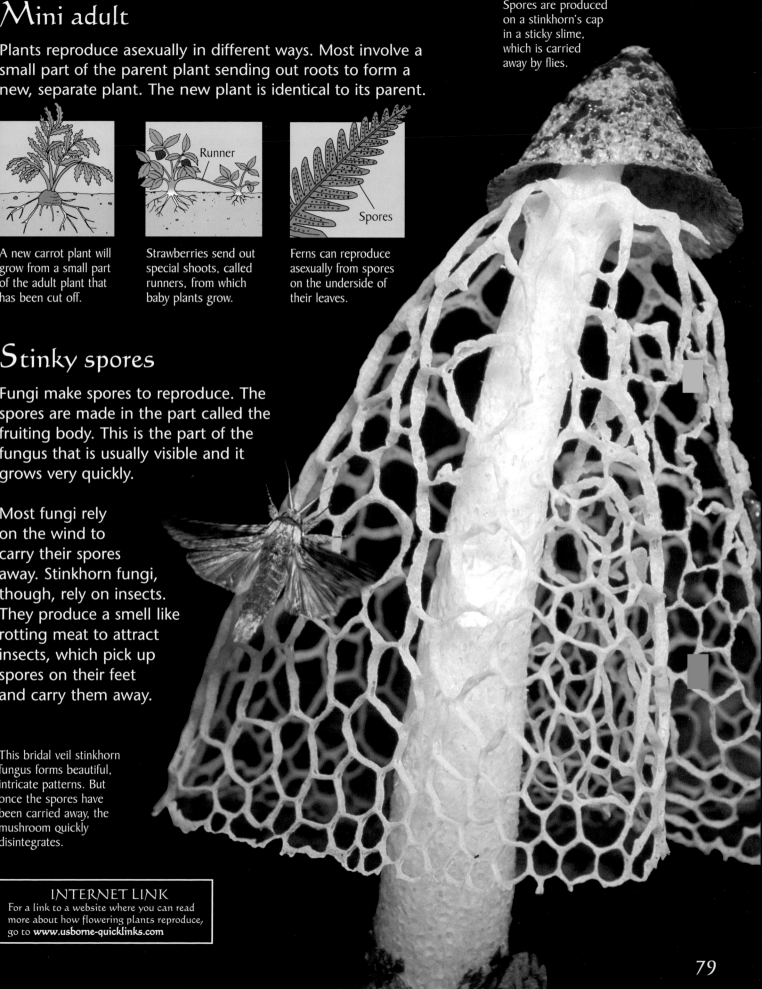

A new carrot plant will grow from a small part of the adult plant that has been cut off.

Strawberries send out special shoots, called runners, from which baby plants grow.

Runner

Ferns can reproduce asexually from spores on the underside of their leaves.

Spores

Stinky spores

Fungi make spores to reproduce. The spores are made in the part called the fruiting body. This is the part of the fungus that is usually visible and it grows very quickly.

Most fungi rely on the wind to carry their spores away. Stinkhorn fungi, though, rely on insects. They produce a smell like rotting meat to attract insects, which pick up spores on their feet and carry them away.

This bridal veil stinkhorn fungus forms beautiful, intricate patterns. But once the spores have been carried away, the mushroom quickly disintegrates.

Spores are produced on a stinkhorn's cap in a sticky slime, which is carried away by flies.

INTERNET LINK
For a link to a website where you can read more about how flowering plants reproduce, go to www.usborne-quicklinks.com

OCEAN OFFSPRING

Ocean creatures have fascinating solutions to the problems of finding a mate and bringing up young. But for some, parental responsibility ends as soon as the eggs are laid.

Mates for life

When a male anglerfish bumps into a female in the depths of the ocean, he clings on and never lets go. He receives all his food from her, through a shared blood supply. The arrangement means that she always has a male available to fertilize her eggs. This saves her from having to hunt for a mate in the darkness.

Fickle fish

Cuckoo wrasse, like some other species of fish, can change sex. All cuckoo wrasse are born female, but most change sex and become male as they grow older. If an old male wrasse in a mixed group dies, one of the females will change sex to replace him.

A female cuckoo wrasse

A male cuckoo wrasse

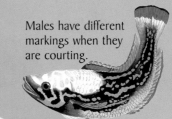

Males have different markings when they are courting.

Two male anglerfish are attached to this large female. She can carry as many as six males. At first, the male grips the female with his teeth. Eventually, his mouth becomes fused to her body.

This fish is hatching from its egg. The blood vessels carry food from the yolk to the fish.

Food supply

Most fish lay eggs which hatch outside their bodies. When the young fish first hatch, they are still attached to the sac of yolk which nourished them while they were inside the eggs. For a few days, this provides them with their own, ready-made food supply.

Deadly dash

Female loggerhead turtles always return to the beach where they hatched to lay their own eggs. Each turtle lays over 100 eggs and buries them in the sand. She lays so many because when the baby turtles hatch, they must rush across the sand to the sea. Many will be eaten by predators, such as sea birds, as they dash to safety.

After hatching, the baby turtles run as fast as they can to the sea.

Big baby

Whales are mammals, which means whale mothers feed their babies on their own milk. Newborn humpback whales are enormous – about 3.5m (12ft) long. They weigh up to two tons. This is as big as a large, well-loaded van. They stay with their mother for about a year.

A newborn whale calf drinks its mother's fat-rich milk.

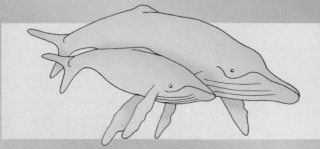

After a year the whale calf has doubled in length.

INTERNET LINK
For a link to a website where you can read about a very modern ocean father – the seahorse, go to www.usborne-quicklinks.com

PARENTAL CARE

Amphibians are creatures that spend time living in the water and on land, at different stages in their lives. Both reptiles and amphibians lay eggs. Some care for their young after they have hatched, feeding and protecting them.

Independent young

Most snakes lay soft, leathery eggs. They must keep them warm and moist for healthy young snakes to hatch. Some snake parents urinate on their eggs to stop them drying out too much. Many snakes look after their eggs before they hatch but leave their babies alone afterwards. A snake gets out of its egg using a sharp tooth on the tip of its snout, called an egg tooth, to slit the shell.

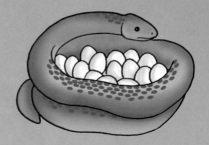

A python lays up to 100 eggs. She coils her body around them to keep them warm.

After three months, they hatch. The mother has lost half her body weight, and is so weak that she can't lay eggs for several years.

A baby snake may stay near its egg for several days after it first breaks the shell, until it feels safe enough to leave.

Backful of babies

Surinam toad mothers keep their eggs safe by carrying them around embedded in the skin of their backs. Baby toads develop completely inside the eggs, so that when they leave their mother, they are immediately able to look after themselves.

Baby toads develop inside the eggs. After three months, they emerge from the skin of their mother's back, looking like miniature adults. They are able to swim and eat right away.

A female Surinam toad lays her eggs on the male's tummy. He fertilizes the eggs and rubs them into her back. After a few days, they sink into the spongy skin, as shown above.

INTERNET LINK
For a link to a website where you can read all about snake love, go to
www.usborne-quicklinks.com

Devoted mother

Baby crocodiles hatch from their eggs looking like small versions of their parents. They call to their mother as they are hatching, to let her know that they are there and need taking care of. She has already guarded her eggs constantly for two months, and continues to look after her young when they hatch. After a few weeks, her babies leave to fend for themselves and find places of their own to live.

This baby crocodile has just hatched.

Land and water

Some salamanders are amphibians. The young ones live underwater. The adults live on land but stay near water because they must lay their eggs in water. These salamanders have a four-stage life cycle, similar to other amphibians such as frogs, toads and newts.

A salamander lays its eggs in water. They are protected by a jelly-like substance which also nourishes them.

Larvae emerge from the eggs. They breathe with gills, and have small legs and long tails. They have teeth and feed on tiny insects.

The larvae develop lungs and can now breathe on land. They still spend most of their time in the water, though.

Adult salamanders walk on land but still have tails. They feed on worms and small insects, and return to water to lay eggs.

EGGS TO CHICKS

All birds lay eggs. An egg is like a womb outside the mother's body, protecting and feeding the chick inside. The advantage of laying eggs is that the mother doesn't have to carry the growing chicks in her body. She can fly around and search for food.

The life of an egg

An egg takes about a day to form inside a bird. The first part to form is the yolk, around the cell that will become the chick. The yolk is the food that will nourish the growing chick. The white forms around the yolk, then finally the shell forms and the egg is laid.

After several weeks, when the chick has used up the yolk and has grown to fill the shell, it is ready to hatch.

This chick is ready to hatch. It has used up all the yolk and fills the shell.

A cold start

Female emperor penguins lay their eggs in the middle of winter. They live on Antarctica, the coldest continent, and face a constant struggle to keep their eggs and chicks warm. If an egg touches the ice, the chick inside will quickly freeze to death.

A penguin keeps its chick warm under a flap of skin on its tummy.

A female lays one egg. She leaves it with the father. He balances the egg on his feet, under a warm flap of skin called a brood pouch.

After about 65 days, the female returns with food for the newly-hatched chick. She now takes care of the chick while the father finds food.

Keeping warm

All eggs must be kept warm, for healthy chicks to hatch. Birds use their body warmth to keep their eggs at the correct temperature, turning them regularly to heat them evenly. This is called incubation.

Most birds have brood patches. These are bare patches of skin where blood vessels run close to the surface. Some birds have a single, large brood patch. Others have separate patches for each egg.

Geese pluck feathers from their chest to make one large brood patch. They save the feathers and use them to line their nest.

Blue-footed boobies keep their eggs warm on their large, webbed feet. When the chicks are nearly able to fly, the parents leave them.

INTERNET LINK
For a link to a website with detailed information about an egg's development, go to **www.usborne-quicklinks.com**

Putting in the time

European robins are helpless when they first hatch. The chicks are tiny, blind and can't fly. They eat almost constantly – parent birds may make hundreds of trips a day to find food for their chicks.

Eggs that hatch quickly tend to produce more helpless chicks. Eggs that need a long incubation before they hatch tend to result in chicks which can look after themselves almost immediately. Either way, eggs and chicks take up a lot of parents' time.

A robin chick signals that it needs to be fed by opening its mouth wide. The inside of the mouth is bright orange or red to show up inside the murky nest.

MAMMALS' MILK

Mammals spend more time than any other animals caring for their young. Mammal mothers feed their babies on milk, which they make inside their bodies. The babies depend on this until they can eat other food. They may spend months or years with their mothers.

Long-term love

After a nine-month pregnancy, a female orang-utan gives birth to one baby. The baby drinks its mother's milk until it is six or seven years old. Even after the young orang-utan has stopped drinking milk, it stays in its mother's care for another few years. Finally, at the age of about ten, it leaves its mother and can fend for itself.

For the first four months of an orang-utan's life, it clings to its mother's front and feeds on her milk.

After four months, the baby begins to eat soft fruit, given to it by its mother. It still drinks milk as well.

Orang-utans usually live alone, but males and females come together to mate. After that, the female will take care of their baby for up to ten years.

Fast food

When Weddell seals are born, they must build up a layer of fat quickly to survive the Antarctic cold. To do this, they drink their mother's fatty milk. Weddell seals' milk is about 60% fat (compared to cows' milk, which is about 4% fat). Within a week, a pup is fat enough to take to the water. It doubles its weight in ten days.

A Weddell seal pup is born small and slim, in contrast to its fat mother. She is as round as a barrel. The pup begins to suckle right away.

The newborn pup feeds constantly. After a month, the pup is plump and well-fed but its mother is skinny and exhausted.

Eggs and milk

Platypuses belong to an odd group of mammals called monotremes, which are egg-laying mammals. Monotremes have many mammal-like features, such as furry bodies and the ability to feed their young with milk. They also have reptile-like features, though, such as laying leathery eggs instead of giving birth to live young.

When the eggs hatch, the babies drink milk. It oozes out of two patches of skin on the mother's tummy.

INTERNET LINK
For a link to a website where you can find out more about mammals' milk, go to www.usborne-quicklinks.com

A female platypus lays her eggs in an underground nest and incubates them on her tummy, with her tail curled around them.

Six months after birth, a joey's weight has increased by about 2,000 times.

First journey

Wallabies are mammals with pouches, called marsupials. A wallaby gives birth to her baby, or joey, after it has spent only 28 days in her womb. It is tiny and helpless, so it crawls up her fur from the birth opening to find her pouch, where it stays for the next few months.

When it is bigger, it leaves the pouch for short periods. After about a year, the joey stops drinking its mother's milk and leaves the pouch for good.

A joey crawls up to the mother's pouch from her birth opening. It is blind and about the size of a rice grain.

Inside the pouch, the joey sucks milk from its mother's nipple.

NEW GENERATIONS

Some insects go through amazing changes during their development from egg to adult. In the middle stages, their bodies may not resemble the adult insect at all.

This photo has been adapted to show three stages of a butterfly's life cycle at once.

INTERNET LINK
For a link to a website all about butterflies and their life cycles, go to www.usborne-quicklinks.com

A newly-emerged swallowtail butterfly waits for blood to flow into its wings before it can fly away.

Changing shape

A butterfly goes through four stages during its life cycle.

The chrysalis looks a little like a dead leaf. This protects it from being eaten.

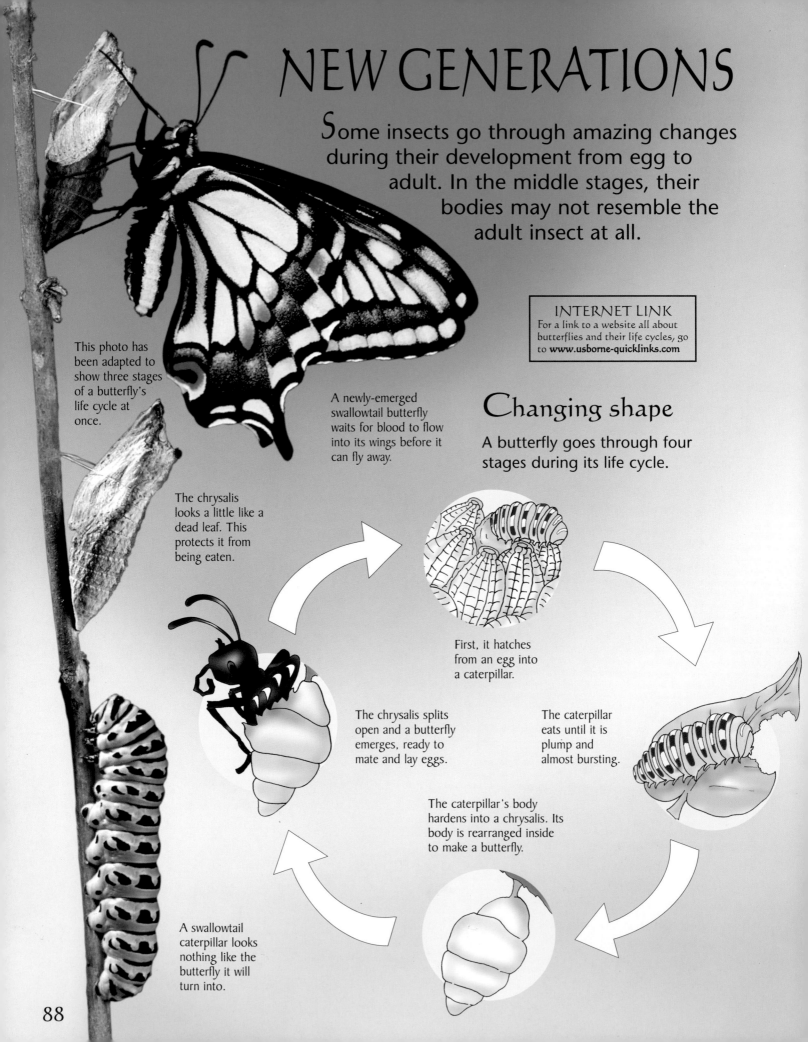

First, it hatches from an egg into a caterpillar.

The chrysalis splits open and a butterfly emerges, ready to mate and lay eggs.

The caterpillar eats until it is plump and almost bursting.

The caterpillar's body hardens into a chrysalis. Its body is rearranged inside to make a butterfly.

A swallowtail caterpillar looks nothing like the butterfly it will turn into.

88

Baby boom

Aphids have a complicated life cycle which involves sex change and having babies without mating. This allows them to reproduce very quickly during the summer. If all the aphids descended from a single female in one summer were lined up end to end, they would stretch more than four times around the Earth.

This female aphid is giving birth to a live daughter.

Female aphids hatch from eggs on a host plant. They give birth to daughters which soon have their own babies, without mating.

The aphid population explodes. The aphids feed on the host plant. They may weaken or even kill the plant.

Some aphids grow wings and fly to different plants to feed. But as summer ends, aphids return to their original plant species.

At the end of the summer, some aphids become male. They mate with the females, who lay eggs, which will form the next generation.

Shedding skin

Young locusts, called nymphs, grow quickly when it is warm. Their skin doesn't grow with them, though. As they get bigger, they shed their skin several times. Locusts have a three-stage life cycle – egg, nymph and adult.

A female locust digs a hole to lay her eggs in. Nymphs hatch, looking like tiny, wingless adults.

A nymph eats constantly and grows quickly. It sheds its skin several times before becoming an adult.

By the time it is an adult, the locust has wings and is ready to fly away and mate.

PLANT INTRUDERS

Some plants don't grow in soil in the usual way. Instead, they grow on other plants. This is because they can't make enough – or any – food for themselves, so they steal it from a plant that can. Plants that do this are called parasitic plants.

Fleeting flower

The biggest flower in the world is the rafflesia. A single flower may measure up to 1m (36in) across. Rafflesia is a parasitic plant which has no stem, roots or leaves of its own. It feeds by breaking into the roots of a tropical vine. It spends most of its life hidden underground and only flowers for a short time.

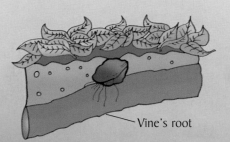

Vine's root

A rafflesia seed lands on the ground near the roots of a tetrastigma vine. The seed sends tiny threads into the vine's roots to feed itself.

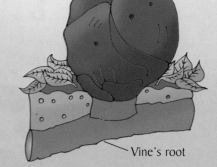

Vine's root

After about 18 months, the rafflesia forms a bud on the ground near the base of the vine. It grows up to 16cm (6in) across.

INTERNET LINK
For a link to a website with more information about the rafflesia, go to **www.usborne-quicklinks.com**

Nine months after a bud forms, it flowers. The flower has thick, fleshy petals and gives off a strong smell which attracts flies to pollinate it. After a few days, it rots into a black slime.

Piggy back plant

Mistletoe grows on tree branches. It uses its own green leaves to make food but also saps nutrients from its host. Many mistletoe plants may grow on a single tree. Mistletoe doesn't usually kill the tree, though, because if the tree dies, the mistletoe will die too.

A mistletoe seed, dropped by a bird, takes root on a branch and starts to grow.

The plant sends suckers into the tree's bark to sap extra nutrients. It also makes its own food using sunlight.

Birds eat the mistletoe's berries, which contain its seeds. The seeds pass out in the birds' droppings. Some land on new tree branches and grow there.

Dark invaders

Squawroots have no green leaves, and can't make their own food using sunlight. Instead, they break into the roots of oak or beech trees to steal their nutrients. Because they don't need sunlight to grow, they can survive in complete shade, or even when buried by leaves fallen from their host tree.

Squawroots grow in North America. They are often eaten by hungry bears that have woken from their winter sleep.

These squawroots are covered in flower buds and have small, scaly, brown leaves.

PLACES TO STAY

The ocean floor is a varied seascape and there are swift currents up near the surface. Below and above, creatures find places to hide and ingenious ways to stop themselves being swept away.

Coral caves

Coral reefs are full of cracks and crevices, which make good hiding places for fish such as moray eels. These lurk in caves during the day with only their heads poking out, snapping at fish that swim by. Their skin blends in with the coral. At night they come out of hiding to hunt for prey in the dark.

This moray eel is lying in wait with its jaws gaping, ready to snap up passing fish. Even the inside of its mouth is camouflaged against its hiding place.

INTERNET LINK
For a link to a website with a sea otter webcam and other otter information, go to **www.usborne-quicklinks.com**

Night anchor

Sea otters have an original way to stop themselves drifting away from their family when they go to sleep. They wrap themselves up in long ribbons of a seaweed called kelp. Sea otters live in large family groups, hunting by day for sea urchins, which they crack open with rocks. They never leave the water.

Kelp grows up from the sea bed in long strips, which the otter wraps around its body.

Lawn of eels

Garden eels live in colonies on the sea floor. They bury their back ends in the sand and let their heads drift. They feed on tiny ocean creatures, called plankton, that float by on the gentle currents.

A moray eel is stealthy enough to make a surprise attack on a colony of garden eels.

A colony of garden eels resembles an underwater lawn, swaying in the ocean currents.

If danger threatens, a garden eel can retreat into its burrow with lightning speed.

Coral cities

Coral polyps are tiny creatures that build hard skeletons underneath themselves. They can withdraw into their skeletons but spend most of their time outside, catching plankton to eat in their waving tentacles.

Many types of coral polyps live close together in their millions and form reefs. But some, like the cup coral below, live alone.

This cup coral has caught a small fish in its stinging tentacles. Its skeleton base is very large, at around 1cm (0.5in) across.

FITTING IN ANYWHERE

Most animals live mainly on land or in water and their bodies are adapted accordingly. Amphibians, though, are equally at home in either place.

Water and land

Amphibians such as frogs, toads, newts and some salamanders, have lungs and must breathe air. But they also take in oxygen through their moist skins, both from the air while they are on land, and underwater. They have powerful legs and are superb swimmers. This gives them advantages underwater when it comes to escaping predators and hunting for food.

If a frog is threatened by a land predator, it dives into the water to escape. It has webbed feet for serious swimming.

Frogs feed on water creatures like insect larvae and fish. If food in the water is scarce, they hop back onto land for a meal of insects, spiders, snails and worms.

This amphibian, called a fire-bellied newt, spends most of its time in the water. It comes onto land to rest or to bask in the sun.

This picture shows a close-up view of a hellbender's wrinkled skin.

Streambed salamander

Hellbender salamanders make their homes underwater, at the bottoms of rivers. Their bodies are flattened so currents rush over them, instead of sweeping them away. They live under rocks, blending into the background and hunting by stealth. They eat anything they can swallow.

A hellbender breathes through its skin, which is wrinkled to give a greater surface area.

All at sea

Sea snakes are reptiles, like land snakes, but they have some special features that allow them to spend their entire lives at sea. Their bodies are slightly flattened and they have paddle-shaped tails to help them swim. Sea snakes can dive up to 100m (110yd) to search for food. But usually they stay in shallower water, so that they can easily come to the surface to breathe.

A sea snake has special valves over its nostrils, that close to keep the water out when it is diving.

A sea snake can take in enough air to stay underwater for about two hours between breaths.

One long lung, shown in yellow, runs the entire length of a sea snake's body.

INTERNET LINK
For a link to a website where you can find out more about all different kinds of amphibians, go to
www.usborne-quicklinks.com

Tree house

Tree snakes have long, thin bodies and wide belly scales to grip tree trunks. All tree snakes have extremely strong muscles, which they use to help them climb. Some have backbones and muscles strong enough to support half their body, anchored by the other half wrapped around a branch. This allows them to reach for prey across slender, widely-spaced branches.

To climb a thin tree, a tree snake wraps its back end around the trunk and reaches higher up the tree with its head.

When its front end has managed to get a good grip, the tree snake pulls up the back part of its body to follow.

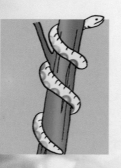

To climb a tree that is too wide to wrap itself around, a tree snake slithers up the trunk as if it were on the ground, gripping with its wide belly scales.

NEST BUILDING

Birds build nests in places where their eggs and chicks will be safe from predators and the hazards of the environment. Some nests hide their occupants. Others are built high up, to keep eggs and chicks out of harm's way.

Joint effort

Great blue herons nest in colonies at the tops of trees or on cliff ledges. Each male heron chooses a nest site and defends it from other males. He might build a new nest from scratch or repair an existing one.

The male heron searches for sticks and twigs. He brings them to the female and she builds the nest.

A heron pair takes up to a week to make a nest solid enough for the female to lay her eggs. They continue to add sticks after the eggs hatch, to strengthen it.

INTERNET LINK
For a link to a website where you can look
at webcams of birds' nests, go to
www.usborne-quicklinks.com

A weaver bird starts a nest by
tying a strip of grass in a knot
around a branch. It then
adds to it gradually.

Hidden contents

Weaver birds build intricately
woven nests. They are made of
grasses, which the male bird tears into
strips, then knots and weaves together
using his beak and claws. The nest has a
downward-facing entrance, which helps
protect the mother and chicks from hawks and
snakes. But some hawks feel the nests with their
feet, to find out if there are eggs or chicks inside.

Tucked-up safe

African penguins dig nest
burrows. They hollow them
out of soil, or piles of other
birds' droppings. The
burrows protect their eggs
and chicks from predators,
and also shelter them from
the hot sun. The main threat
to the chicks is from a
burrow collapsing.

Fairy feet

Fairy terns don't build a nest at all. They just perch their
egg on a tree stump or piece of driftwood, in a dent on a
tree branch, or even in the fork where two branches meet.
The chick hatches complete with oversized feet that can
grip its perch, however precarious.

This fairy tern chick was
hatched in a high place. It
hangs on tight with its
large feet.

It takes about two weeks for a penguin to
make a burrow. Instead, they may shelter
in burrows dug by other birds or animals.

A PLACE TO SLEEP

Mammals need safe places to sleep. Not many can risk sleeping out in the open, especially young ones. Most make temporary or permanent shelters from materials they find nearby.

Different dens

For most of the year, adult foxes sleep and take shelter wherever they can. This might be in a hollow tree, under a rock or even curled up in a drainpipe. They rest during the day and come out at night to hunt.

When they have a family, though, some foxes dig an underground den. The female stays inside the den, guarding the pups, while her partner hunts for food.

These foxes are using a rocky crevice as a temporary den to shelter in.

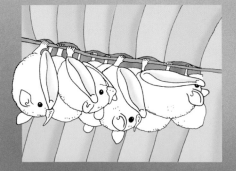

A fox's underground den may have many chambers and several entrances.

Camping out

Some rainforest bats make their own safe places to sleep, in tents made from leaves. The bats chew along leaf veins to make folds in a leaf, then sleep inside the tent this creates. A leaf tent can last for up to a year.

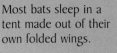

Most bats sleep in a tent made out of their own folded wings.

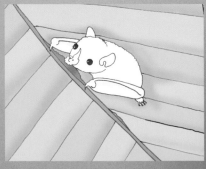

A bat starts to make a leaf tent. It bites holes in the leaf with its teeth to make it droop.

The two sides of the leaf form a tent. Up to 15 bats might roost under a single banana leaf tent.

Lazy life

Koalas live in and feed on eucalyptus trees. But leaves don't provide much energy so they spend about 80% of their time asleep, curled up in the fork of a branch.

When they are awake, they are either feeding or just sitting still. They only come down to the ground to move to a new tree.

INTERNET LINK
For a link to a website where you can find out more about tent-making bats, go to www.usborne-quicklinks.com

A koala sleeps, clinging onto a tree branch with its sharp claws.

Secret entrance

Beavers live in families consisting of two parents and their young, in a home called a lodge. The only way to get into the lodge is by swimming underwater to reach its entrance. This means that the family can sleep safely there, protected from predators such as wolves and bears.

Beavers use their long front teeth to chop down trees.

They use wood and mud to dam streams and form lakes.

The lodge is a pile of sticks and branches in the middle of the lake.

99

INSECT PALACES

Many kinds of insects build homes using materials they can find easily, such as wood or mud. Some make an amazing team effort to build enormous structures for their colony, thousands of times larger than the insects themselves.

Massive mound

Termites build taller structures than any creature apart from humans. Their huge mounds are ventilation shafts, which provide fresh air for the underground nests beneath. Some mounds are over 12m (39ft) high.

Termite mounds are made of mud and saliva. Some are shaped like umbrellas to shed rain water.

Little lodgers

Slender ants live inside the thorns of acacia trees. This provides them with shelter and food. In return, the ants sting animals that might try to eat the tree. Slender ants share their thorny home with scale insects. These suck the plant's juices and make a sweet substance, called honeydew, which the ants feed on.

Scale insect

Cocoon containing a developing ant larva

Ant

Here you can see slender ants, ant larvae and scale insects covered in sticky, white honeydew.

INTERNET LINK
For a link to a website where you can discover all the insects living in a single tree, go to www.usborne-quicklinks.com

This ant is carrying a cocoon to a different part of the nest.

Self-build colony

A paper wasp queen starts to build her nest in spring, after spending the winter tucked up in a crack or crevice. The nest houses her new colony of female workers. It only lasts for one summer. She then dies. The next year, a new queen will start another nest.

The young wasps that emerge will form a new colony.

She lays an egg in each cell. Larvae will hatch and develop in the cells.

The queen wasp builds a nest of wood and saliva, made of six-sided cells.

Leaf home

Leaf-mining caterpillars live inside leaves, eating them from the inside. This is the juiciest part of a leaf and the easiest to digest. The leaves also protect the growing caterpillars from predators and the weather. When the caterpillars change into moths, they fly away.

This leaf is scarred with curving patterns where caterpillars have eaten tunnels inside it.

A TOUGH LIFE

Some plants have special features that allow them to grow in places that are too hot, dry or cold for other plants. Still, even these plants can be damaged or killed by really unusual weather conditions.

Some deserts have so little rain that these flowers may only bloom every five years.

Reacting to rain

Cacti have fleshy stems that expand to store water after any rain in the desert. Their roots collect water from near the surface of the ground, before it drains away. They flower after rain, producing seeds for the next generation before drought sets in again.

Cactus spines are actually very thin leaves, with a small surface area so they don't lose much moisture.

Seed survival

Desert soil is full of seeds. There may be hundreds in a handful. Some flower within hours of beginning to grow after rain. The blooms last a few days, then the plants die. Some deserts are so dry that there may be many years between flowerings – but the seeds can survive the wait.

Part-time leaves

Ocotillo plants survive in very dry conditions by only coming into leaf when there has been heavy rain. Their stems have green parts that can make food for the plant using sunlight, so it does not need to have leaves all the time – they would only provide more area for water loss.

For most of the year, an ocotillo looks like a bunch of dead sticks. One plant has up to 75 stems, with spines along their length.

Immediately after rain, the ocotillo bursts into leaf. The fleshy leaves grow in bunches. The plant also flowers every year.

The ocotillo's flowers are red and tube-shaped. Their shape means they can only be pollinated by hummingbirds.

Branching out

Joshua trees are shaped by the weather. If the temperature in the desert drops below freezing, flowers form at the growing tips of the plant. After flowering, the plant branches off in a new direction. If there are no flowers, no branches form and the plant grows straight up.

Joshua trees grow slowly – about 2cm (1in) per year. A single plant lives for around 200 years, on average, but some are up to 1,000 years old.

Cold start

A tiny alpine snowbell starts growing while there is still snow covering the ground. This means it is ready to push its flowers into the open as soon as the snow starts to melt. This in turn means that its flowers can produce seeds before larger plants grow and crowd it.

The snowbell starts to grow from a seed while there is still snow on the ground. It pushes up beneath the snow.

As soon as the snow melts, the delicate flower breaks through to the surface.

Joshua trees are not really trees at all – they are a kind of large yucca plant.

INTERNET LINK
For a link to a website where you can find out about a kind of algae that turns snow red, go to www.usborne-quicklinks.com

SEA MONSTERS

The deep sea is home to some weird, wonderful and terrifying creatures. They have found ways to cope with their surroundings – the temperature, the changing pressure and the almost complete lack of light to see by.

Looking up

Hatchet fish skulk around in deep waters, shrouded in darkness. They have upturned eyes to spot smaller fish silhouetted above, and attack unexpectedly, from below. A hatchet fish has lights which can be dimmed or brightened to blend in with light from above, making it hard to see from deeper down in the depths.

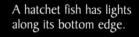

A hatchet fish has lights along its bottom edge.

The hatchet fish's mouth is upturned, for scooping up prey. The fish is only small, about 3–5cm (1–2in) long.

Monster squid

A real deep-sea monster is the giant squid. Scientists think they grow as long as 30m (100ft) – and possibly even longer. None, though, have ever been seen alive in their natural habitat. Instead, gruesome clues to their existence turn up occasionally, like the body of one washed ashore, or the sucker-scarred skin of a sperm whale.

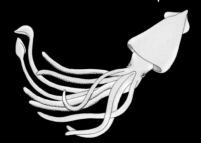

Giant squids live in the murky depths. Their bodies function best in cold water.

Sperm whales have been found with giant squid sucker wounds on their skin.

Vicious viperfish

A viperfish is a deep-sea predator, with long, needle-like teeth. Its prey can't see it coming – the ocean depths are too dark. It is designed to be able to swallow anything it comes across. The fish's lower jaw is hinged, so it can swallow large victims. Most of its organs are near the head. The rest of its body is just an expandable tube, for digesting all sorts of prey.

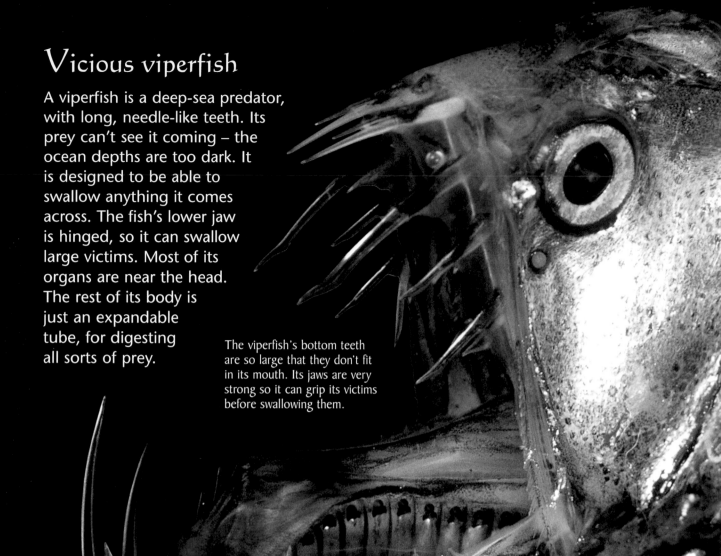

The viperfish's bottom teeth are so large that they don't fit in its mouth. Its jaws are very strong so it can grip its victims before swallowing them.

INTERNET LINK
For a link to a website which provides a fascinating glimpse of life in the abyss, go to **www.usborne-quicklinks.com**

This viperfish may look terrifying, but it is only 25cm (10in) long.

Hot home

Where deep-sea water seeps into a crack or vent in the ocean floor, it is heated by red-hot rocks. The water near the vent is cold – around 2°C (36°F) – but the water in the vent is very hot – around 375°C (707°F). Some creatures can survive these extreme temperatures.

Hot, chemical-filled water gushes out of a vent, looking like a plume of black smoke. Tubeworms, clams and crabs cluster around the opening.

Tubeworms have feathery tops that absorb minerals from the water. Bacteria use these minerals to make food for the tubeworm. In return, the bacteria get a safe place to live, near the vent.

Some kinds of ghostly white crabs are able to survive in the extreme temperatures near the vent. They nibble on the tubeworms.

COOK OR CHILL

A few reptiles and amphibians are able to stand extreme heat or cold. Some can even survive droughts which would dry out and kill other creatures.

A lizard rests on its belly to cool all four feet.

Too hot to handle

Frogs, like other amphibians, need to stay moist to survive. During hot, dry months, an Australian water-holding frog burrows into the ground and goes to sleep. This is called aestivation. It is similar to hibernation, which means sleeping through the coldest months of the year.

INTERNET LINK
For a link to a website with amazing thermal images of warm and cold-blooded creatures, go to www.usborne-quicklinks.com

This water-holding frog is at the bottom of a stream — an ideal, moist environment for an amphibian.

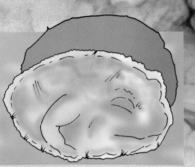

Inside its burrow, a water-holding frog curls up inside a cocoon made of its own shed skin. This seals water near its body.

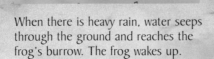

When there is heavy rain, water seeps through the ground and reaches the frog's burrow. The frog wakes up.

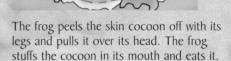

The frog peels the skin cocoon off with its legs and pulls it over its head. The frog stuffs the cocoon in its mouth and eats it.

106

Keeping cool

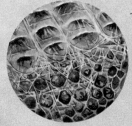

Surface temperatures in the desert can reach 65°C (150°F). Fringe-toed lizards lift each foot in turn to cool them down enough to walk on them. If it still feels too hot, the lizard dives below the surface of the sand, where it can stay for up to 24 hours.

Sand diving is also how the lizard escapes from predators. But if it rains while the lizard is above ground, the sand gets too hard for the lizard to burrow, and it is trapped.

The lizard lifts each foot in turn to cool them.

Keeping it in

Crocodiles bask in the sun to keep warm but the heat could also dry them out. To avoid this, their skins are almost waterproof, to seal water in. The large scales on a crocodile's back (which receives more sun than its belly) form a completely waterproof barrier. The belly scales are smaller and form a flexible, less waterproof surface which allows the crocodile to move.

The large scales on a crocodile's back are like shields, sealing water in. The belly scales don't need to provide as much protection from the sun, as they are shaded most of the time.

Deep freeze

A few reptiles and amphibians, including some frogs, toads and turtles, can survive cold winter temperatures by hibernating. Some burrow below the level of frost in the ground or stay underwater. Others, like the wood frog, can cope with being partly frozen. Up to one-third of the wood frog's body fluid freezes solid, but its vital organs stay working all winter to keep it alive.

A crocodile basks in the sun. It may get very hot but it never sweats, as this would dry its body out.

As cold weather approaches, the wood frog burrows into the leaf litter on the forest floor.

The top layers of ground freeze during winter and the frog freezes with them. Its body systems slow down while it hibernates.

BIRD EXTREMES

Birds have many special features that help them cope with everyday life. Some have more extreme conditions to cope with than others – dealing with intense cold, for instance, or living in permanent darkness.

An Arctic tern has long wings but very short legs, as it spends so much of its time in the air.

Extremely far

Arctic terns spend the brief Arctic summer breeding and raising young. Then they fly south to the Antarctic, to feast on krill in the Southern Ocean. Like many migrating birds, they follow the ocean winds and rarely touch down on land. In a year, each tern completes an average round trip of 35,000km (22,000 miles).

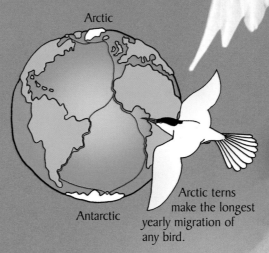

Arctic

Antarctic

Arctic terns make the longest yearly migration of any bird.

INTERNET LINK

For a link to a website with lots of information about penguins, go to www.usborne-quicklinks.com

Penguin chicks huddle together to fight the cold. They take turns standing near the edge of the group.

Extremely cold

Emperor penguin chicks are born in winter and are well able to cope with the Antarctic cold. They have thick, downy coats and are extremely fat. For extra warmth, the chicks huddle together in large groups called crèches, while their parents go fishing. By the time the chicks take their first swim, the weather is warmer. It's not so far to walk to the sea, either, since as sea ice melts, the edge of the water creeps closer.

Extremely fast

The fastest flying bird on record is the peregrine falcon. It uses gravity to help it make dizzyingly fast dives, called stoops, and knock its prey out of the sky. It can reach speeds of over 160kph (100mph). Incredibly, it is still able to steer at this speed. If it misses the first time, it can pull up and attack from beneath. A human fighter pilot changing direction as suddenly as this would probably lose consciousness.

A falcon climbs above a pigeon in the air, then goes into a fast dive.

The falcon hits the pigeon so hard that it kills it immediately.

Extremely dark

During the day, oilbirds roost deep inside pitch dark caves. They make loud clicks and listen to the echoes bouncing off objects around them to find their way.

At night, they leave their caves and use their keen sense of smell to find ripe fruit trees. They also have excellent vision to help them fly through the dark forests.

Navigation by listening to echoes is called echo location. Other creatures that use it include dolphins and bats.

HEATING AND COOLING

Mammals' bodies stay at a steady temperature but they can still feel the cold or heat. They have different ways of dealing with harsh climates.

Thermostat ears

Black-tailed jackrabbits live in deserts, where temperatures swing between extremes of hot and cold. At night, the temperature drops, and the jackrabbit's long ears lie along its back to save heat and keep its body warm. During the hot, sunny days, its ears stick straight up, to give off heat.

A jackrabbit's ears keep the chill off its body at night. Folding them flat helps keep heat from escaping.

The ears are full of blood vessels. Wind passing across them cools the blood flowing close to the surface.

In hot water

Japanese macaques live on mountains that are covered in snow and ice during winter, when the temperature drops as low as -10°C (14°F). They have thick fur and hug each other to keep warm. A few lucky macaques live near natural hot springs. The macaques bathe in the steamy, volcanic pools to keep warm.

Outside the warmth of the pool, the macaques' fur quickly gets covered in snow and ice.

Furry feet

Snowshoe hares have very long, furry feet, which help to keep them from sinking in deep snow. Even the sides of the feet and the gaps between the toes are covered in fur. If the snow is very soft and powdery, a hare will spread all four toes on each back foot, to make a larger surface area.

The snowshoe hare is only white during winter. When spring arrives and the snow melts, its coat begins to turn brown for better camouflage.

INTERNET LINK
For a link to a website with a webcam showing snow monkeys bathing in a hot pool, go to www.usborne-quicklinks.com

Hay hoarders

Pikas live in places where the summers are warm but the winters are icy, with little food. In summer, they gather grass and pile it under sheltered rocks, where air dries it out. A pika gathers a big enough food supply to last it through the coming winter.

Each pika makes its own haystack and guards it fiercely.

Big dippers

Rhinos live in hot, grassland areas, with little shade from the burning midday sun. They search for food early in the day when it is cooler. Later on, they spend their time wallowing in mud. This cools the rhinos down and the mud helps to keep the sun off their skin. It also protects them from biting insects.

Rhinos prefer to forage for grasses, fruit and leaves during the early morning, before the day becomes too hot.

During the afternoon, rhinos go to streams or swamps, where they spend hours wallowing in mud to keep cool.

TINY PIONEERS

Insects and other creepy-crawlies can live in places where no other animals are able to survive. They also live in great numbers wherever there are people, feeding on the scraps we leave behind.

Sturdy springtails

Springtails are microscopic creatures that are able to survive Antarctica's freezing temperatures. They live in places where the ground is not usually covered in ice, such as inland valleys. A special liquid in their blood prevents their body fluids from freezing.

Springtails are preyed on by even tinier mites. But they can escape quickly.

They use their tails to flick themselves away from danger.

Catching fog

The Namib Desert is extremely dry, with hardly any rain. Most water arrives in the form of nighttime fog which blows inland from the nearby Atlantic Ocean. Fog-basking darkling beetles collect this water to drink, by angling their bodies in the direction of the incoming fog. Droplets of water condense on their shiny wing cases and trickle down to their mouths.

The beetle does a kind of handstand so that any drops of water on its back run down to its mouth.

Bowled over

Wheel spiders living in the dunes of the Mojave Desert use the sandy slopes to help them escape from predators. If a wheel spider feels in danger, it curls up into a ball. It can then simply roll away down the face of a sand dune, much faster than either it, or its attacker, could run.

A wheel spider can't move very fast over the slippery desert sand.

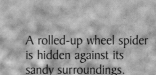

If threatened, it folds its legs underneath itself and prepares to roll away from danger.

A rolled-up wheel spider is hidden against its sandy surroundings.

INTERNET LINK
For a link to a website with lots of fascinating cockroach facts, go to
www.usborne-quicklinks.com

In warm, tropical climates, cockroaches can grow as big as the one in this photograph.

Rampant roaches

Cockroaches live on every continent except for Antarctica. They are so widespread because they can eat almost anything, from bat-droppings to book-bindings. They can also survive in a range of temperatures – but not below freezing. When it gets too cold, they might move into people's houses.

TAKING CONTROL

Plants can't react to their surroundings by walking, running or making noises. But they can grow in particular ways, control the amount of water they take in, or curl up and hide. Scientists can even give plants special built-in survival features using genetic engineering.

Growing up

Mushrooms are the reproductive parts of certain fungi. Spores grow in the gills – the flaps that line the underside of the mushroom's cap. As a mushroom grows, it pushes up. Once it is free of the surface it expands to open its gills. The gills hang down, so the spores fall out between them and are carried away by the wind to new homes.

Spores drop down and are blown away.

Disappearing leaves

The mimosa plant has a clever way of dealing with a grazing animal. Instead of letting itself be eaten, it quickly hides its juicy leaves by folding them away, in the hope that the animal will lose interest and leave it alone.

Mushrooms growing out of a tree trunk adjust their direction of growth so that the gills hang straight down.

Normally, a mimosa is bushy – attractive to a grazing animal like a cow.

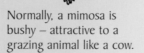

At the slightest touch, the leaves fold up and look less appetizing.

If the cow persists, whole branches droop to reveal prickly thorns on the stem.

114

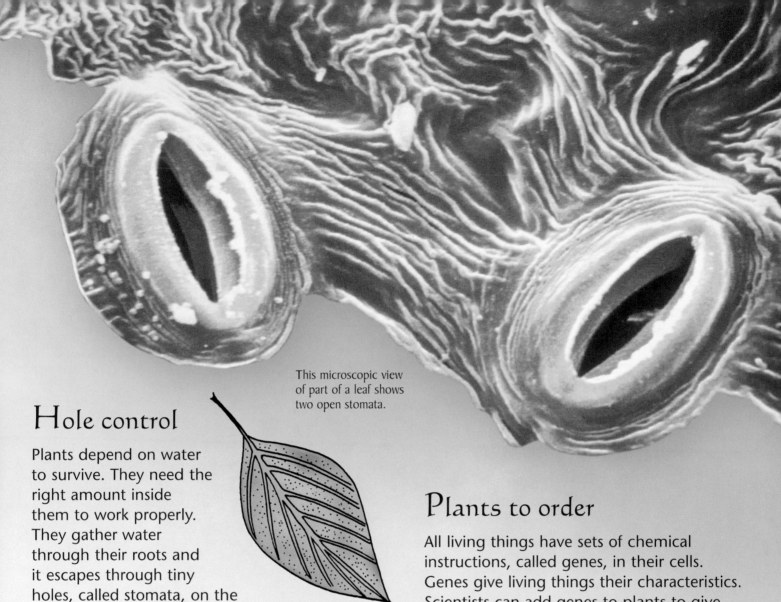

This microscopic view of part of a leaf shows two open stomata.

Hole control

Plants depend on water to survive. They need the right amount inside them to work properly. They gather water through their roots and it escapes through tiny holes, called stomata, on the underside of their leaves.

When the plant contains enough water, its cells are swollen and the stomata stay open. They let water out. If the plant doesn't have enough water, its cells become floppy. Then the stomata are closed, so no more water is lost. They also close at night.

Most stomata are found on the underside of a plant's leaves, as shown by the green dots.

Plants to order

All living things have sets of chemical instructions, called genes, in their cells. Genes give living things their characteristics. Scientists can add genes to plants to give them different characteristics. For instance, plants can be grown that are more resistant to disease or pests. Plants adapted in this way are said to be genetically engineered, or genetically modified.

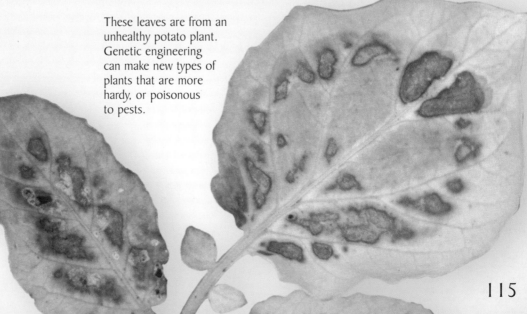

These leaves are from an unhealthy potato plant. Genetic engineering can make new types of plants that are more hardy, or poisonous to pests.

INTERNET LINK
For a link to a website all about the issues surrounding GM crops, go to www.usborne-quicklinks.com

PARTY TRICKS

Sea creatures have some special ways to catch prey and shake off enemies. Sharks use electrical impulses to seek out their prey. Hagfish tie themselves in knots to get away. One cunning octopus even does impersonations of other creatures.

A mimic octopus can look like a poisonous flatfish...

...or a venomous lionfish with spines outstretched...

...or even a highly poisonous sea snake, by burying six of its legs.

Adaptable octopus

The mimic octopus is a recently discovered creature, capable of looking like several other, more dangerous, creatures in order to escape predators. It does this by arranging its arms and body in different ways to change shape.

Slimy surprise

Hagfish are long and thin, and look similar to eels. They have a secret weapon that they use to fend off predators – slime. The slime is released from glands along the sides of a hagfish's body. It is made of proteins and sugars, and is thick, stringy and elastic. It forms a protective coating around the hagfish.

If it feels threatened, a hagfish can suddenly produce an enormous amount of slime which coats its body.

The hagfish can also tie itself in a knot which it moves along its body. This is useful for cleaning off old slime.

Dropping arms

A brittlestar feeds by burying itself in sand, up to the base of its arms. It waves these in the water to catch tiny creatures, which it moves to its mouth in the middle of its body. But the waving arms also attract fish, which nibble them or try to tug the brittlestar free of the sand. It is able to let part, or all, of an arm snap off. A new arm will grow from the stump.

All the brittlestar's organs are contained within the central part of its body. This explains how it can lose arms and still survive. In this photograph, the brittlestar is perched on some red coral.

Sensitive shark

All sharks have sensitive organs that pick up the electrical signals given off by other creatures in the water. But hammerhead sharks have wide, hammer-shaped heads, which are covered in these organs for extra sensitivity. They can even detect rays buried under the sandy sea floor.

Hammerhead sharks also have an especially good sense of smell, for seeking out prey. They have a nostril on each end of the hammer. This allows them to decide what direction a scent is coming from, and so track down their prey.

This is the last view an unfortunate ray might see – a hammerhead shark coming in for the kill, having detected its heartbeat.

A hammerhead shark swims along the sea bed, moving its hammer from side-to-side in a sweeping motion.

It detects the ray's heartbeat from under the sand. The shark scoops the ray out of its hiding place and eats it.

A hammerhead's eyes and nostrils are on the ends of its hammer.

INTERNET LINK
For a link to a website where you can find out more about sharks' senses, go to **www.usborne-quicklinks.com**

EXTRA FEATURES

Some reptiles and amphibians use special senses or sneaky tricks to help them survive. Extra senses may allow a reptile to hunt in the dark, for instance, or taste its surroundings. Creatures have surprising ways of making a quick getaway, too.

Heat seeker

Pit vipers have special sensory organs just in front of their eyes which can detect tiny changes in temperature – as little as 0.003°C (0.005°F). A viper follows heat sources to seek out warm-blooded prey, such as rodents. This extra sense means that the snake doesn't need vision to track its prey. It can hunt at night, or even deep down in dark burrows.

The pits just in front of the viper's eyes, on either side of its face, are heat-sensing organs.

Pit

Extra eye

Tuataras are reptiles, with a body design that has stayed unchanged for millions of years. They live in New Zealand, and are capable of withstanding much lower temperatures than other reptiles – as low as 12°C (54°F). Perhaps their most amazing feature is a hidden eye, which is completely covered by skin.

A tuatara may use the third eye as a daylight sensing device, because it can probably detect sunlight. The eye has a lens, and there is even a hole in the skull in front of it, but this is completely covered by skin and scales.

Third eye is under here.

A heroic tail

Many lizards' tails break off easily, if they are attacked. It is better for a lizard to survive without a tail than to be eaten. A tail is a useful piece of lizard equipment, though – it helps it to balance – and so sometimes, a lizard will grow a replacement tail.

INTERNET LINK
For a link to a website where you can find out about some really amazing animal senses, go to www.usborne-quicklinks.com

Muscles in the tail stump contract around the wound to prevent too much bleeding.

Tasting the air

Nile monitors, like other lizards and snakes, use their tongues to taste the air. They flick their forked tongues in and out, picking up tiny scent particles from the air. These particles are rubbed over the entrances to a sensitive organ inside the lizard's mouth. This helps the lizard to identify other animals nearby – prey or perhaps a possible mate.

A Nile monitor lizard flicks its tongue in and out to sense its surroundings.

On a roll

Mount Lyell salamanders are perfectly equipped for getting around their rocky home, on the slopes of the Sierra Nevada mountains in North America. They have webbed feet which cling to the steep, rocky surfaces. They also use the tip of their tail like an extra leg to help them climb. If they feel threatened, they simply roll away down the slopes to safety.

If it is touched, the Mount Lyell salamander will curl up into a ball.

The salamander rolls and bounces down the mountain, unable to control its direction.

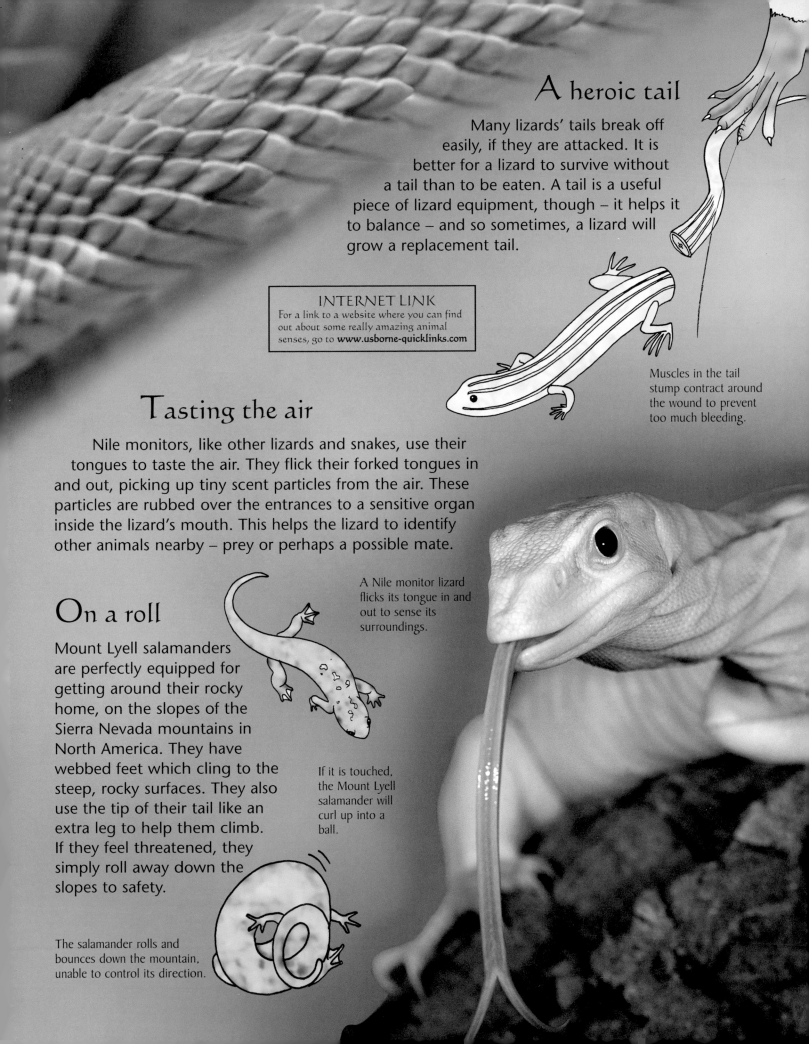

SIGHT AND FLIGHT

Sight is vital to most birds, to help them catch prey. Birds have huge eyes, packed with special cells to give them sharp sight. Another feature that all birds share is a coat of feathers to keep them warm, dry and help them to fly.

Non-stop sight

Birds of prey depend on their excellent vision to spot and catch prey. Most have a transparent film, or membrane, that regularly moves across the surface of each eye, to keep them clean and moist. This means that the birds don't often need to blink with their eyelids, so they don't lose vital seconds of sight during the chase.

Near the back of this hawk's eye you can just see the edge of the transparent film that keeps it clean and moist.

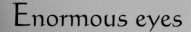

A hawk keeps its eyes fixed on its prey from the moment it spots it.

Enormous eyes

Compared to the size of their heads, birds' eyes are many times larger than humans'. An owl's eyes are so enormous that there is no room left in its head for muscles to move the eyes. It must move its whole head to look in a different direction. It can turn its head around by 180° to look behind itself. The eyes are also packed with cells called rod cells, which help it to see very well in dark or dim light.

An owl can see in light that is 100 times poorer than people can see in.

Fabulous feathers

The feathers that birds use to fly have a central shaft with a flat vane either side. The vanes are made of barbs which hook together. This structure is strong, light and flexible – all the features which make it possible for birds to fly. Feathers also give birds a warm and waterproof covering.

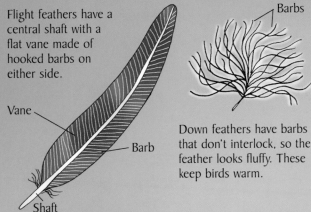

Flight feathers have a central shaft with a flat vane made of hooked barbs on either side.

Vane

Barb

Shaft

Barbs

Down feathers have barbs that don't interlock, so the feather looks fluffy. These keep birds warm.

The photograph on the right shows a magnified view of a swallow's feather, showing the hooks, called barbules, which lock the barbs together.

INTERNET LINK
For a link to a website featuring champion birds – the highest, the fastest and the oldest – go to www.usborne-quicklinks.com

Solar power

Roadrunners have their own built-in solar panels to make the most of the Sun's energy. During the cold desert nights, a roadrunner rests. But when the Sun rises, the bird soaks up its rays through a black patch of skin on its back. By warming itself thoroughly, it can gather enough energy to run very quickly after prey.

When a roadrunner is fully warmed up, it can reach speeds of over 24kph (15mph). It chases lizards, snakes and even hummingbirds.

SUPER SENSES

Many mammals have one, highly developed sense or special ability which helps them survive. This might be one of the five senses that we have or it could be an extra, sixth sense.

Half asleep

Dolphins live in water but breathe air. They must decide to come to the surface every time they need to take a breath. They also need to sleep for a certain amount of time every day. So that they get enough rest, and still remember to breathe, dolphins sleep with only half their brain at a time. The other half stays awake, to decide when to breathe.

Starring nose

Most moles use their sense of touch to get around underground and seek out prey. A star-nosed mole has a snout ringed by extremely touch-sensitive tentacles. These twitch constantly, helping the mole to feel its way through the darkness and find food.

A dolphin sleeps with one eye closed. The other is alert to possible danger.

It sleeps just below the surface of the water. Its bones are light so it doesn't sink.

Every few minutes, it flips its tail and rises to the surface. It opens its blowhole to let out stale air and take in fresh.

When the mole finds food, the tentacles on its snout fold back out of the way while it eats. It has huge claws to shovel soil out of its way.

Each one of a tarsier's eyes weighs more than its tiny brain. The eyes are 1.6cm (0.6in) across.

Super-size eyes

Tarsiers are small mammals that live in trees and hunt at night. They have the largest eyes, compared to their body size, of any animal. They need to be able to see their insect prey in the dark. Because the eyes are so big, they don't move in their sockets. Like owls, tarsiers can turn their heads around to see behind them.

A tarsier can twist its head 180° in either direction, like an owl.

INTERNET LINK
For a link to a website about nocturnal creatures, go to **www.usborne-quicklinks.com**

Freezing with fear

If it is extremely frightened, an opossum may pretend to be dead. Its act can be so convincing that a predator, such as a fox or a dog, will leave it alone. The predator seems to believe that the opossum really is dead, even when it has been moving around normally only moments before. An opossum can stay completely still for up to four hours, if necessary.

If an opossum is threatened by a predator, it may run, growl, belch or even urinate to try to scare the predator away.

If it is completely terrified, it freezes. It rolls over, lets its tongue hang out, becomes stiff and hardly breathes.

A predator may be fooled into thinking the opossum is dead. Preferring live meat, it will usually leave the opossum alone.

TINY BUT AMAZING

Insects have very small bodies but they pack in some incredible features. Silk, one of our most luxurious fabrics, is made from threads produced by moth caterpillars. Another type of insect has a drill on its body that can penetrate wood. Insects have powerful senses, too.

Male moths use their feathery antennae to pick up the scent of females.

Feathery feelers

Moths usually fly at night, using their long antennae to smell their way around. The antennae are feathery and covered in tiny hairs, to increase their surface area. This makes them extremely sensitive. As well as smell, the antennae detect movement. Moths mainly use them to find food and to follow the scent of a possible mate.

Each branch of an antenna is covered in sensitive hairs. The antennae can detect a female moth over 1.5km (1 mile) away.

INTERNET LINK
For a link to a website where you can get a real bee's eye view of things, go to **www.usborne-quicklinks.com**

Many eyes

Most insects have compound eyes. These are made up of thousands of single eyes. Some dragonflies have up to 30,000 eyes in their compound eyes. Each single eye provides a different image, which merges with the others to give the insect one large, fragmented view.

Compound eyes can't move or focus, but are probably able to detect movement.

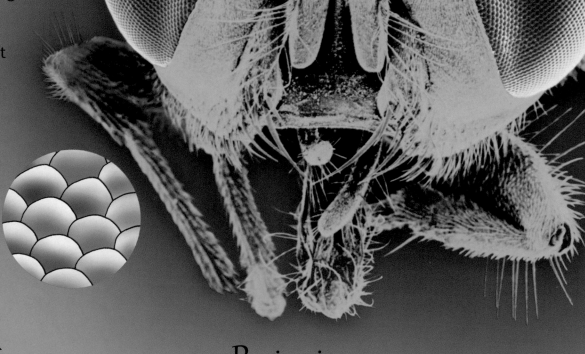

Each single eye in a compound eye is called an ommatidium. It has a lens and a cone of cells behind which make an image.

Spinning silk

Silkworms make their cocoons out of long, silk threads. Over four thousand years ago, people found that these threads could be collected and woven to make silk fabric. Silk makes beautiful clothes. It is light and very strong, but also soft and luxurious.

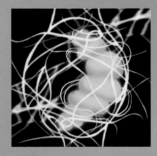

A silkworm caterpillar begins to make a silk cocoon. It spins the silk into a long, continuous thread, using a spinneret on its lip.

The caterpillar changes into a moth inside the cocoon. The moth dissolves one end of the silk cocoon with saliva, then comes out.

Boring insects

Ichneumon wasps lay their eggs inside the bodies of wood-boring insect larvae. The wasps track down larvae by sensing the vibrations made as they chew through wood. A wasp uses a long tube to drill through the wood and into the larva to lay its eggs. Scientists think the tube may be tipped with a kind of metal that makes it hard enough to bore through wood.

The tube is stored inside a sheath.

Tube

An ichneumon wasp drills into the bark of a tree. The tube may be up to 7.5cm (3in) long.

INDEX

The numbers shown in **bold** type show where major subject areas are covered.

ACKNOWLEDGEMENTS

Every effort has been made to trace the copyright holders of the material in this book. If any rights have been omitted, the publishers offer to rectify this in any future edition, following notification. The publishers are grateful to the following organizations and individuals for their contribution and permission to reproduce this material.

Cover (front) (m) ©Barbra Leigh/CORBIS, (b) ©Joe McDonald/CORBIS, (background) ©Digital Vision; Cover (back) ©Digital Vision; Endpapers ©Digital Vision; 1 ©Andre Seale/Alamy; 2–3 ©NHPA/Stephen Dalton; 5 ©NHPA/Stephen Dalton; 6 ©David Aubrey/CORBIS; 7(b) ©Naturfoto Honal/CORBIS; (tl) ©Farrell Grehan/CORBIS; 8 ©Amos Nachoum/CORBIS; 9(mr) ©Fred Winner/Jacana/Science Photo Library; 10 ©David A. Northcott/CORBIS; 11(t) ©David A. Northcott/CORBIS; 12 ©Steve Kaufman/CORBIS; 12–13(main) ©Kim Taylor/Bruce Coleman Collection; 14 ©Gallo Images/CORBIS; 15 ©Randy Wells/CORBIS; 16 ©Joe McDonald/Bruce Coleman Collection; 17 ©Gary Vestal/Bruce Coleman Collection; 18 ©Kevin Schafer/CORBIS; 19 ©Robert Pickett/CORBIS; 20 ©Jonathan Blair/CORBIS; 21 ©F.S. Westmorland/Science Photo Library; 22–23(main) ©Joe McDonald/CORBIS; 23(br) ©NHPA/Stephen Dalton; 24–25(main) ©Roy Morsch/CORBIS; 25(tr) ©Bob & Clara Calhoun/Bruce Coleman Collection; 26–27(b) ©Getty Images/Mitchell Funk; 27(m) ©Adam Jones/Bruce Coleman Collection; 28–29(t) ©Dr. John Brackenbury/Science Photo Library, (b) ©Martin Dohrn/Science Photo Library; 30 ©Getty Images/Angelo Cavalli; 31 ©Lester Lefkowitz/CORBIS; 32 ©DY Riess MD/Alamy; 33 ©Getty Images/Steven Hunt; 34 ©Roy Toft/National Geographic Image Collection; 35 ©Getty Images/Oliver Strewe; 36 ©Mary Ann McDonald/CORBIS; 37 ©Wolfgang Kaehler/CORBIS; 38 ©John Conrad/CORBIS; 39 ©Kevin Schafer/CORBIS; 40 ©Eye of Science/Science Photo Library; 41 ©Anthony Bannister, Gallo Images/CORBIS; 42 ©Martin Harvey, Gallo Images/CORBIS; 43 ©Dr Jeremy Burgess/Science Photo Library; 44 ©Jeffrey L. Rotman/CORBIS; 45 ©Getty Images/Mark Conlin; 46 ©Digital Vision; 47 ©Getty Images/Steve Satushek; 48–49(t) ©David A. Harvey/National Geographic Image Collection; 49(b) ©Wolfgang Kaehler/CORBIS; 50 ©John Conrad/CORBIS; 51(b) ©Digital Vision; 52 ©Darlyne A. Dr. Murawski/National Geographic Image Collection; 53(t) ©Buddy Mays/CORBIS; (b) ©Chris Mattison, Frank Lane Picture Agency/CORBIS; 54(l) ©Neil Lucas/Naturepl; 55 ©Art Wolfe/Science Photo Library; 56(b) ©Jeffrey L. Rotman/CORBIS; 57(tr) ©ImageState.com; 58 ©Norbert Rosing/National Geographic Image Collection; 59(t) ©Whitehead, Fred/Animals Animals/Earth Scenes; 60 ©Clem Haagner, Gallo Images/CORBIS; 61 ©Lynda Richardson/CORBIS; 62 ©NHPA/Haroldo Palo Jr; 63 ©Dr Karl Lounatmaa/Science Photo Library; 64 ©Ralph A. Clevenger/CORBIS; 65(t) ©Michael & Patricia Fogden/CORBIS, (b) ©George D. Lepp/CORBIS; 66 ©Getty Images/Gail Shumway; 67(t) ©Claude Nuridsany & Marie Perennou/Science Photo Library, (b) Wolfgang Kaehler/CORBIS; 68(tl) ©Getty Images/Steven Hunt; 68–69(b) ©Digital Vision; 69(t) ©Getty Images/Gary Bell; 70–71(b) ©Getty Images/Kevin Schafer; 71(t) ©George Grall/National Geographic Image Collection; 72 ©Willis, Gladden William/Animals/Earth Scenes; 73 ©Michael S. Yamashita/CORBIS; 74 ©David Kjaer/Naturepl; 75 ©Anup Shah/Naturepl; 76(b) ©Australian Picture Library/Leo Meier; 76–77(t) ©Digital Vision; 78(t) ©Jonathan Smith, Cordaiy Photo Library Ltd/CORBIS, (b) ©Digital Vision; 79 ©Kevin Schafer/CORBIS; 80 ©Getty Images/Peter David; 81(t) ©Anthony Bannister, Gallo Images/CORBIS; 82 ©David A. Northcott/CORBIS; 83(t), (ml) ©David A. Northcott/CORBIS, (mr) ©Martin Harvey, Gallo Images/CORBIS; 84(tr) ©Robert Pickett/CORBIS, (b) ©Tim Davis/CORBIS; 85 ©Roy Morsch/CORBIS; 86 ©Getty Images/ Manoj Shah; 87 ©Martin Harvey, Gallo Images/CORBIS; 88 ©Gray Hardel/CORBIS; 89 ©NHPA/ G. Bernard; 90 ©John Holmes, Frank Lane Picture Agency/CORBIS; 91 ©Gary W. Carter/CORBIS; 92 ©Royalty-Free/CORBIS; 93 ©Jeffrey L. Rotman/CORBIS; 94 ©Chris Mattison, Frank Lane Picture Agency/CORBIS; 95 ©Stephen Frink/CORBIS; 96 ©Joe McDonald/CORBIS; 97(t) Getty Images/Laurence Hughes, (b) ©Kennan Ward/CORBIS; 98 ©Torleif Svensson/CORBIS; 99 ©Martin Harvey, Gallo Images/CORBIS; 100–101(main) ©Anthony Bannister, Gallo Images/CORBIS; 101(br) ©Anthony Bannister, Gallo Images/CORBIS; 102 ©William Manning/CORBIS; 103 ©Royalty-Free/CORBIS; 104 ©Paulo De Oliveira/OSF; 105 ©Paul A. Zahl/National Geographic Image Collection; 106 ©Chris Mattison, Frank Lane Picture Agency/CORBIS; 107 ©Martin Harvey, Gallo Images/CORBIS; 108(t) ©Digital Vision; 108–109(b) ©Getty Images/Wolfgang Kaehler; 110(b) ©Tom Brakefield/CORBIS; 111(t) ©Tom Brakefield/CORBIS, (br) Michael S. Quinton/National Geographic Image Collection; 112 ©Michael Fogden/OSF; 113 (m) ©Michael & Patricia Fogden/CORBIS, (br) Richard T. Nowitz/CORBIS; 114 ©Getty Images/Christoph Burki; 115(t) ©Andrew Syred/Science Photo Library, (b) ©Patrick Johns/CORBIS; 116 ©Peter Scoones/Oliver Strewe; 117 ©Jeffrey L. Rotman/CORBIS; 118–119 ©Frank Lane Picture Agency/CORBIS; 119 ©David A. Northcott/CORBIS; 120(t) ©Levin, Ted/Animals Animals/Earth Scenes, (b) ©Digital Vision; 121 ©Andrew Syred/Science Photo Library; 122(t) ©Digital Vision, (b) ©Habicht, Michael/Animals Animals/Earth Scenes; 123 ©Dick, Michael/Animals Animals/Earth Scenes; 124 ©John Mitchell/Science Photo Library; 125(t) ©NHMPL/Science Photo Library, (b) ©OSF/Animals Animals/Earth Scenes.

Illustrators:
Ian Jackson, David Quinn, Chris Shields and Nigel Frey.

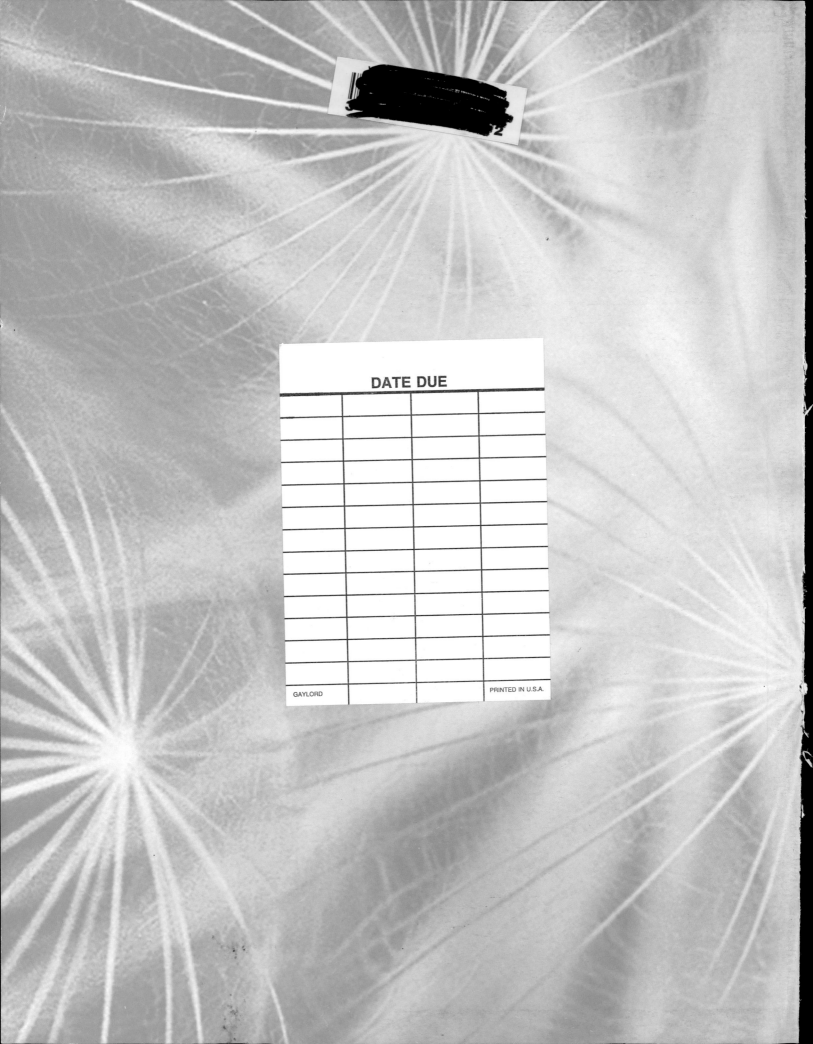

DATE DUE
